Quick Bytes:

Computer Lover's Cookbook

By Diane Pfeifer

Illustrations by Clark Taylor

Published by Strawberry Patch, Atlanta, Georgia

ISBN: 0-9618306-7-0
Library of Congress Number: 93-083442

Published by:
Strawberry Patch
P.O. Box 52404
Atlanta, GA 30355-0404
(404) 261-2197

First Edition

Editor: Diane Pfeifer
Design & Composition: Paula Chance, Diva Designs, Atlanta, GA
Mac Input: Jeff Justice
Printing: Gilliland Printing Co.
Binding: Prizma Bindery
Author Photo: Brian Dougherty

*This book is an Equal Opportunity Effort, composed on a PC and
designed on a Mac. Any "BIOS" towards either system is purely unintentional.
All recipe titles and cartoons are intended as parodies
and are not meant to infringe on any trademarks.*

This book is dedicated to
my husband Jeff Justice and daughter Jennica Snow
who put up with me data-to-data.

I would like to thank all software companies for
their confusing manual terminology
and most of all, I thank God
for giving me a *really* productive way to use it.

❀   ❀   ❀   ❀   ❀   ❀

Bundles of thanks to:
David Leonard, my original computer guru
Dan Poynter and PMA for self-publishing support
Raj Singha for DOS-aster diverting
The Atlanta PC User's Group
The Sai Baba Center for recipe sampling

Dear Fellow Users,

Whether computer nut or novice, you'll enjoy this fun mix of bytes and bites. Although I composed my first two cookbooks on a computer, I didn't become a "nerd" until I tried writing a database to run my book publishing business.

After months of dbf files, relational data, string expressions and the like, I decided to make edible use of this terminology now permanently stored in my brain. Thus "Quick Bytes: Computer Lover's Cookbook" was born.

Since true computer lovers would rather be on line than in the kitchen, these prompt, user-friendly recipes will make those necessary evils (cooking and eating) a breeze. Some recipes need a bit of preparation time but cook fast, while some are the reverse — but either way your time off line is minimal. And all recipes are vegetarian for those users who wouldn't dream of hurting a "mouse".

Bytes Wishes,

Diane Pfeifer

P.S. Enjoy the book and remember: No eating or drinking near your keyboard!

❋　　❋　　❋　　❋　　❋　　❋

About the author:

Diane Pfeifer is the author and publisher of two best-selling cookbooks, *For Popcorn Lovers Only* and *Gone With The Grits*. Her previous careers include chemistry, singing, songwriting for such artists as Debby Boone and Paul Anka, and recording wrong numbers for the phone company. She is a PC lover compatibly married to a Mac user, comedian Jeff Justice. Their 4-year-old daughter Jennica uses both systems, wisely keeping her preference a secret.

Table of Contents

• • • • • •

Tech Support

Glossary

* * * * * *

Accelerator	:Microwave
Access denied	:Diet time
Alt	:As in "alt and pepper to taste"
ASCII	:Callii tech support
Autoexec.bat	:Cookies in your boss' car
Backslash	:Do to piecrust before baking
Backup	:Leftovers
Basic	:PBJ sandwich
Batch	:Mess o'
Binary	:Buy nary, eat nary
Block	:Cake baked with no eggs
Bomb	:Bomb
Boot	:Heat your oven
Cache	:Do when egg is rolling off counter
CAD	:Someone who promises to cook, then doesn't
CD	:When you don't core apples before baking
Cluster	:Kitchen advisers
Command	:Tell someone else to cook
Compress	:Knead
Config.sys	:Have your sister figure it out
Copy	:Double recipe
Crash	:Drop main course at big dinner party
Ctrl	:What you lose after crashing
Cursor	:Who you are after crashing
Customize	:Add sprinkles
Data	:Sort-a like-a fig-a
Debug	:Check the flour before using
Dip-switch	:What you do when you're out of salsa
Directory	:De place where de priest lives
Document	:Small, after-dinner candy
DOS	:Dine Or Starve
Dot matrix	:Dorothy's mother
Download	:Pour batter into pan
Downtime	:Time while brownies are baking
Drag	:Time while brownies are baking
Enter	:Put in oven

Escape	:Order out
Expansion	:Too much yeast
Export	:Take leftovers to the neighbors
Extract	:Usually vanilla
F.A.T.	:See "Access denied"
Fastopen	:Do to oven when you overbake
Floppy	:Bake longer next time
Folder	:Blender
Fragment	:What's left of brownies
Freeze	:Do when you accidently quadruple the recipe
Giga-byte	:Enough for an army
Goto	:As in "Goto restaurant when recipe bombs"
Help	:Julia Child
High density	:Forgot to fold in the eggs
Highlight	:Top with white icing
Icon	:I con cook anything better than you con
Import	:Borrow a cup of sugar
Interface	:Where a lady puts her dinner
Laptop	:Eat only the icing

Loadhigh	:Put in freezer
Log on	:Cook in the fireplace
Logic	:Why somebody else should cook
Loop	:Why somebody else thinks you should cook
LPT1	:Put on front burner
Mainframe	:Oven
Meg	:Mc chickens lay 'em
Mega-byte	:Slow down!
Mega-hertz	:When you forget to use a potholder
Memory	:Forget it — use a timer
Menu	:Surely you're kidding
Merge	:Nickname for margarine
Microchips	:Serve with micro salsa

Modem	:Top with ice cream	Scanner	:Guest deciding whether to eat
Monitor	:Oven window		
Mono	:One-burner stove	Scroll	:Recite list of ingredients
Motherboard	:Mom's tired of cooking	Select	:Choose edible portion
Nanosecond	:Time it takes to eat DOS-Serts	Serial	:What you eat when you make a bomb
Nerd	:Someone who understands this whole glossary	Shareware	:Mom's crock pot
Network	:I slice, you dice	Shift	:"Cap" cake with icing
Norton	:Maybe he'll fix these recipes for you	Sort	:Pick the burnt ones out
Parameters	:Kitchen doors	Spreadsheet	:Use under really messy cooks
Parse	:Nickname for parsley	Tab	:Drink after "Pie A La Modem"
Password	:"Dinnertime"	Tech support	:Hello, Mom?
Path	:Worn-out place leading to refrigerator	Toggle	:Switch recipes
		Turbo	:High setting on microwave
Postcript	:Dessert		
RAM	:Overeat	VGA	:Add food coloring
ROM	:Overeat in England	Zoom	:I can see it on the table now

Chapter 1
Appe-Byte-Zers

Block Bean Dip

Serves 24-36 users

1	15-ounce can black beans, drained	8	ounces grated sharp cheddar cheese
1/2	teaspoon cumin		Chopped cilantro for garnish, optional
1/4	teaspoon salt		Taco chips or small flour tortillas
1/4	cup chopped onion		
16	ounces sour cream		

In blender or food processor, blend black beans, cumin and salt until smooth. In glass bowl or baking dish, layer bean mixture, chopped onion, sour cream and grated cheese. Top with cilantro, if desired.

Serve with taco chips or small flour tortilla halves.

F.A.T. Reducer: Use lowfat sour cream and lowfat cheddar cheese.

Sidekick

5.0 Layer Taco Dip

● ● ● ● ● ● ● ● ● ●

Serves 24-36 users

16	ounces sour cream	1	cup tomatoes, chopped and well drained
2	tablespoons taco seasoning mix	2	bunches green onions, chopped
2	small ripe avocados	1	9-ounce can no-lard bean dip
1	tablespoon lemon juice	8	ounces sharp cheddar cheese, grated
1/2	cup mayonnaise		Tortilla chips
1	6-ounce can black olives, chopped		

Combine sour cream and taco seasoning. Refrigerate several hours. In separate bowl, mash avocados and blend with lemon juice and mayonnaise. In another bowl, combine olives, tomatoes and onion.

In glass bowl or baking dish, layer ingredients as follows: bean dip, avocado mixture, sour cream, olive/tomato mixture, cheese. Serve with tortilla chips.

F.A.T. Reducer: Use lowfat sour cream and cheddar cheese.

Hotkey Shortcut: Chop black olives in food processor.

I Meg-Plant Dip

Makes about 2 cups

1	medium eggplant	5	tablespoons fresh lemon juice
3/4	cup tahini (sesame paste)	1/2	teaspoon cumin
4	cloves garlic, peeled		Paprika
1	teaspoon salt		Finely chopped parsley

Puncture eggplant with knife and place in baking dish. Broil 4 inches from flame for 20 minutes. Turn occasionally. Remove and allow to cool. Peel off skin.

In blender or food processor, blend tahini, garlic, salt and lemon juice until smooth. Add eggplant and cumin and blend again. Place in serving bowl and sprinkle lightly with paprika. Garnish with parsley.

Clip Art-ichoke Dip

Serves 16-24 users

1	10-ounce can seasoned bread crumbs	2	cloves garlic, crushed
2	14-ounce cans artichoke hearts, juice reserved		OR
		1/2	teaspoon garlic powder
	Juice of 2 lemons	1/8	teaspoon cayenne pepper or to taste
1	cup olive oil		Salt to taste
1	cup grated Parmesan cheese		

Boot oven to 350 degrees F. Mix bread crumbs, artichoke liquid, lemon juice and olive oil in large bowl. Blend artichokes in food processor or blender until finely minced. Mix artichokes into bread crumb mixture.

Add cheese, garlic and cayenne pepper, mixing well. Place into buttered 2-quart casserole. Bake for 20-30 minutes. Serve with Melba toast, crackers or celery sticks.

Cream Cheese Scroll-Ups

Makes 45-60

2	8-ounce packages cream cheese, softened	1/2	teaspoon garlic powder
2	tablespoons green onion, chopped	1/2	teaspoon salt, optional
1/2	cup black olives, chopped	8	medium-sized flour tortillas
1/2	cup shredded cheddar cheese		Salsa for dipping

In food processor or mixing bowl, blend or beat cream cheese until creamy. Stir in onion, black olives, cheese, garlic powder and salt, if needed. Spread thin layer of mixture on tortilla.

Tightly roll up tortilla. Wrap individually in plastic wrap. Refrigerate at least 3 hours or overnight. To serve, cut into 3/4-inch slices. Serve with salsa.

F.A.T. Reducer: Use lowfat cream cheese.

You can bet your "boot" on these!

Data Cream Dream Spread

● ● ● ● ● ● ● ● ● ●

Makes about 3 cups

2	8-ounce packages cream cheese, softened	2	tablespoons ground cinnamon
3	tablespoons milk	1-1/2	cups finely chopped fresh or dried dates

In mixer or food processor, beat cream cheese, milk and cinnamon until creamy. Add dates and blend again. Serve with sliced fruit or crackers.

ALT: For a unique flavor, add 2 teaspoons curry powder and blend.

F.A.T. Reducer: Use lowfat cream cheese.

Del-viled Egg-heads

Makes 24

12	hard-boiled eggs, peeled	2	tablespoons celery, finely minced
2-3	tablespoons mayonnaise		
1	tablespoon Dijon mustard	2	tablespoons green onion, finely sliced
1/2	teaspoon black pepper		
1/2	teaspoon paprika	1	tablespoon red pepper, finey minced
2	tablespoons sweet relish		

Slice eggs in half lengthways. Gently scoop out yolks. Place yolks, mayonnaise, mustard, black pepper and paprika in mixing bowl. Mix thoroughly until creamy. Stir in remaining ingredients.

With rounded teaspoon, stuff egg whites with filling. Sprinkle with paprika. Use any extra filling for quick sandwiches.

Everyone will want to download this dip.

Guaca-Modem Dip

Makes about 3 cups

3	ripe avocados, peeled and seeded		Jalapeño pepper to taste, seeded and finely chopped
1/2	small onion, finely chopped	1/4	cup chopped cilantro leaves
2	tablespoons fresh lime juice		Salt to taste
1	clove garlic, crushed		Chili powder to taste
1	medium tomato, diced		Tortilla chips for dipping

In medium bowl, roughly mash avocado with a fork. Stir in remaining ingredients. Set aside for a few minutes to enhance flavors. Serve with tortilla chips.

Hotkey Totsy Chutney

* * * * * * * * * *

Makes about 1 cup

1	tablespoon ginger root, grated		Juice of 2-3 lemons
1/2-1	teaspoon hot green chilies, minced	1	teaspoon powdered caraway seeds
1	heaping teaspoon sugar		Salt to taste
3	tablespoons cashews	2	bunches cilantro leaves

Place all ingredients (smallest amount suggested) except cilantro in food processor or blender. Blend until smooth. Slowly add handfuls of cilantro and continue blending until chutney is smooth.

Add small amounts of any ingredient until desired flavor is achieved. Let sit 2 hours or overnight for flavor enhancement.

* * * * *

Use this hotkey when you want to spice things up in a hurry.

* * * * *

Field

Hum-Mouse Dip

Makes about 2 cups

6	tablespoons fresh lemon juice		Cayenne pepper to taste
1/2	cup tahini (sesame paste)	1	15-ounce can chickpeas, drained and reserved
3	cloves garlic, pressed	1/4	cup chopped parsley, optional
1/2	teaspoon salt		

In blender or food processor, blend lemon juice, tahini, garlic, salt, cayenne and 1/4 cup chickpea liquid until smooth. Add chickpeas, blending to a rough consistency.

If smoother or thinner texture is desired, add more chickpea liquid and blend accordingly. Stir in parsley, if desired.

Mexi-Clone Taco Popcorn

Makes about 9 cups

8	cups popped popcorn
1	cup crumbled tortilla or corn chips
3	tablespoons butter or margarine

2	teaspoons taco seasoning mix or to taste
1/2	cup grated cheddar cheese, optional

Combine popcorn and chips in large bowl. Melt butter in small pan over low heat. Stir in taco mix and remove from heat. Dribble over popcorn. Toss with hands to coat thoroughly. Serve immediately or continue for a cheesy treat.

Spread popcorn mixture on greased baking sheet and sprinkle with cheese. Place under broiler until cheese melts, about 1 minute. Check constantly to be sure popcorn is not burning. Remove and cool before serving.

F.A.T. Reducer: Use diet margarine and 1/4 cup lowfat cheese.

Nano-Nachos

Serves 6-8 users

1-1/2 cups grated cheddar
cheese
Taco seasoning mix to taste
Tortilla chips
1 9-ounce can no-lard bean
dip

Prepared guacamole dip
16 ounces sour cream
Jalapeño peppers, seeded
and thinly sliced

Melt cheese in medium saucepan over low heat. Stir in taco seasoning and mix thoroughly.

Spread tortilla chips with small amount of bean dip and cheese mixture. If softer nacho is desired, microwave or broil until softened. Top with small amounts of guacamole dip and sour cream. Garnish with sliced jalapeños.

F.A.T. Reducer: Use lowfat cheddar cheese and sour cream.

Nut Cheese Log-On

* * * * * * * * * *

Serves 16-24 users

2   *8-ounce packages cream
      cheese, softened*

1   *envelope dry onion soup
      mix*

1/4 *cup chopped red bell
      pepper, optional*

1   *cup nuts, finely chopped*

In mixer or food processor, whip cream cheese until fluffy. Add soup mix and blend again. Stir in chopped pepper, if desired. Place in bowl and let chill in refrigerator for a few hours. Mold into log shape and chill again until firm. Roll in nuts before serving. Spread on crackers.

F.A.T. Reducer: Use lowfat cream cheese.

Upgrade

Microchip Salsa

Makes about 4 cups

1	6-ounce can black olives, drained	2	tablespoons vinegar or lemon juice
2	14-1/2-ounce cans peeled tomato wedges with juice	1	teaspoon garlic salt
			Salt and pepper to taste
1	4-ounce can chopped green chilies	1/2	cup chopped cilantro
			Tortilla chips for dipping
4	green onion tops, chopped		
1	tablespoon olive oil		

In food processor or blender, pulse olives and tomatoes just until chopped. Place in mixing bowl and stir in remaining ingredients except chips. Chill for a few hours or overnight. Serve with tortilla chips.

Spicy Cheese Wafers

Makes 6-7 dozen

1	pound grated extra-sharp cheddar cheese	2	cups flour
5	tablespoons water	3/4	cup finely chopped pecans
1	stick butter or margarine, softened	14-16	drops hot sauce
			Salt, optional

Blend cheese in mixer with water. Add butter and mix. Add flour, pecans and hot sauce. Form into 2 rolls and wrap in wax paper. Refrigerate overnight. Slice very thin.

Bake on greased cookie sheet at 320 degrees F until light brown, approximately 10-12 minutes. Remove from cookie sheet. While still hot, sprinkle with salt, if desired.

Spinach CO-BOLs

Makes about 70

2	10-ounce packages frozen chopped spinach, cooked and drained	6	eggs, beaten
1	large yellow onion, finely diced	1/2	cup Parmesan cheese
3/4	cup butter or margarine, melted	1/2	teaspoon garlic powder
		1/2	teaspoon salt
		2	cups dry herb bread crumbs or stuffing mix

Combine all ingredients in large mixing bowl. Refrigerate until chilled. Shape into marble-sized balls. Place on greased cookie sheet. Bake at 350 degrees F for 20-25 minutes.

Can be frozen before being baked. Thaw about 1 hour before reheating. Reheat at 325 degrees F for 10 minutes.

Popeye's favorite language!

Stuffed Mush-ROM Caps

Serves 6-8 users

8	ounces fresh mushrooms	1	clove garlic, minced
1	tablespoon butter	1/2	teaspoon salt
1	tablespoon olive oil		Pepper to taste
2	tablespoons green onion, finely chopped	1	cup herb stuffing mix
		1/2	cup boiling water
2	teaspoons fresh parsley, chopped		

Wash mushrooms. Remove and save stems. Put caps in shallow baking dish. Heat butter and oil in medium pan. Finely chop stems and sauté with onion until soft. Add parsley, garlic, salt and pepper. Cook for 1 minute.

Stir in stuffing and hot water to make a stiff mixture. Stuff each cap and bake at 350 degrees F for 15 minutes.

Chapter 2
Select Salads

8.0 Layer Potluck Salad

Serves 24 users

1	head iceberg lettuce, broken into small pieces	1	pound thinly-sliced Swiss cheese, cut into 1-inch strips
1	cup celery, sliced	2	cups mayonnaise or ranch dressing
1	10-ounce package frozen green peas, cooked, drained, and cooled	1	cup Parmesan cheese, grated
1	medium Vidalia or mild onion, finely chopped	1	cup soy bacon bits

In 9x13-inch glass baking dish, layer all ingredients except soy bacon bits in order given. Cover tightly with plastic wrap and refrigerate overnight. Before serving, sprinkle soy bacon bits on top. Cut into squares and serve.

F.A.T. Reducer: Use lowfat cheese and lowfat mayonnaise or dressing.

Don't worry, there's a PC for everyone.

Stacker

Bean-ary Salad

Makes about 4 cups

1	16-ounce can red kidney beans, drained	1/4	cup grated Parmesan cheese
1	16-ounce can garbanzo beans, drained	2	tablespoons olive oil
1/2	small red onion, chopped	1/4	cup wine vinegar
1/2	cup fresh parsley or cilantro, chopped	1	teaspoon garlic powder
		1/2	teaspoon black pepper

Combine all ingredients in bowl. Chill and stir before serving to blend flavors.

Config.Caesar Dressing

Makes about 1 cup

3	cloves garlic	1/2	cup grated Parmesan cheese
	Juice of 1 lemon		Dash of Worcestershire sauce without anchovies
1/4	cup olive oil		Salt to taste
1/2	teaspoon coarsely ground black pepper		
1	egg yolk		

In food processor or blender, blend all ingredients until creamy. If thinner consistency is desired, blend in small amount of water.

F.A.T. Reducer: Reduce olive oil to 2 tablespoons.

"ALT 2, Brute?"

Config.sys

Creamy Avo-CAO-O Dressing

Makes about 1 cup

1 ripe avocado, peeled and pitted	1 tablespoon fresh dill or 1 teaspoon dried dill
1 clove garlic, minced	Pinch sugar
1/4 cup water	1/2 teaspoon salt or to taste
1 tablespoon olive oil	2 tablespoons fresh lemon juice
2 tablespoons sour cream or mayonnaise	

In food processor or blender, blend all ingredients until creamy. Use for salads or as a dip for raw veggies.

dBASIL Tomato Salad

Serves 4 users

1	ball fresh unsalted mozzarella cheese packed in water *
2	large beefsteak tomatoes, sliced
1	bunch fresh basil leaves, chopped

Dressing:

3	tablespoons balsamic vinegar (no substitutions)
1	tablespoon Dijon mustard
1	tablespoon honey
1	tablespoon lemon juice
1/2	cup virgin olive oil
	Salt and pepper to taste

Cut fresh mozzarella into 1/4-inch slices. In oval casserole, stagger layers of mozzarella, tomato slices and basil. Mix dressing ingredients thoroughly. Pour over salad and refrigerate for at least one hour to blend flavors.

* Available at Italian markets, gourmet deli shops and farmer's markets.

My sister-in-law Jacqui makes this fabulous dish — the perfect "relational" dinner salad.

Excel-ery Waldorf Salad

* * * * * * * * * *

Serves 6 users

6   stalks crisp celery
2   crisp red apples, unpeeled
    Lemon juice
1/2 cup walnuts

1/2 cup mayonnaise
    Salt and freshly ground
    black pepper

Wash celery in ice-cold water. Pat dry and slice. Core apples and slice. Sprinkle with lemon juice to prevent discoloration. Toss all ingredients in mayonnaise and season to taste.

Lemon Sys-a-me Dressing

* * * * * * * * * *

Makes about 2 cups

1   cup tahini (sesame paste)
1/2 cup lemon juice
1/4 cup olive oil
2-3 tablespoons tamari or soy
    sauce
1/2 teaspoon black pepper

1/4 cup chopped scallion
1-2 large cloves garlic, pressed
    Dash cayenne, turmeric and
    salt, if needed
    Water

In food processor or blender, blend all ingredients together until smooth. Let sit at least an hour or overnight to blend flavors blend and thicken mixture. Thin with a little water, if needed.

ALT: Blend in 1/2 medium green or red bell pepper for flavor variety.

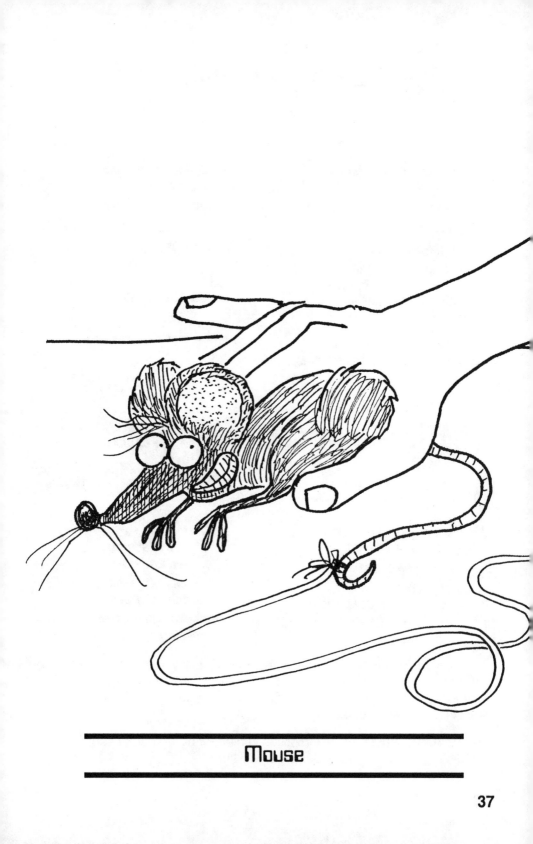

Mouse

Lettuce 1-2-3

Serves 1-2-3 and 4 users

1 head romaine lettuce, washed and dried

2 tablespoons lemon juice

3 tablespoons olive oil

Tear lettuce into small pieces and place in large serving bowl. In small bowl, blend lemon juice, oil, salt, pepper and garlic powder. Toss into salad.

Top each serving with Parmesan cheese and croutons.

Salt and freshly ground pepper to taste

Dash garlic powder

Grated Parmesan cheese

Croutons

"Easy as. . ."

Mac-a-roni Garden Salad

Serves 10-12 users

2 cups snowpeas, stems and strings removed

2 cups cherry tomatoes, halved

2 cups mushrooms, sliced

1 16-ounce can ripe olives, drained and chopped

1 16-ounce package spiral rainbow macaroni, cooked and drained

5 tablespoons grated Parmesan cheese

1 8-ounce bottle Italian dressing

In medium saucepan, place snowpeas in boiling water. Boil for 2 minutes. Rinse in cold water and drain. Place in large bowl. Toss with tomatoes, mushrooms and olives. Stir in pasta, cheese and salad dressing. Chill and serve.

Hotkey Shortcut: Chop olives in blender or food processor by pulsing a few times.

Tab-ouli Salad

2	cups boiling water	1/2	cup minced green onion tops
1	teaspoon salt		
1	cup bulghur (cracked) wheat	1/4	cup olive oil
			Juice of 2 lemons
1	cup minced parsley or cilantro		Salt and pepper to taste
		1	cup chopped tomatoes, optional

Pour boiling salted water over bulghur in medium bowl. Let sit at least 30 minutes to absorb water. Drain off any remaining water. Toss remaining ingredients into the wheat. Stir, mixing thoroughly. Chill before serving, if desired.

ALT: Add 3 teaspoons dried or 2 tablespoons fresh chopped mint leaves for an authentic Middle Eastern touch.

You'll be done in the blink of an I/O.

Reaching the desktop

Chapter 3
Config. Sauces
and Soups

ASCII Broccoli Soup

Serves 4-6 users

4	stalks broccoli, trimmed and chopped	1	teaspoon salt
		3	cups water
1	large potato, peeled and diced	1	envelope dry vegetable soup mix
1	medium yellow onion, chopped	1/2	cup milk

In large soup pot, combine all ingredients except milk. Simmer until broccoli is tender. Place mixture in blender or food processor and blend only until coarsely chopped. Return soup to pot and stir in milk. Heat through and serve.

Curry Cauli-Floppy Soup

Serves 4-6 users

3	cups milk		1	small yellow onion, chopped
1	large head cauliflower, trimmed and chopped		2	teaspoons curry powder
1	large potato, peeled and diced		1/2	teaspoon cumin
				Salt and pepper to taste

Combine all ingredients in medium saucepan. Cover and cook over medium-low heat about 10 minutes until tender. Purée soup in blender. Return to pot and cook 5 more minutes. Serve hot.

ALT: Stir in 1/2 cup grated Parmesan cheese after blending. Heat through.

Adobean Soup

Serves 6-8 users

4	tablespoons olive oil	1	tablespoon dry onion bouillon
1	medium yellow onion, chopped	2	teaspoons ground cumin
1	medium green bell pepper, seeded and chopped	2	teaspoons ground oregano
4	large cloves garlic, crushed	1-1/2	tablespoons wine vinegar
2	cups water	3	15-ounce cans black beans, drained

In large soup pot, heat oil over medium heat. Add onion, green pepper and garlic. Cook until onion is translucent. Stir in remaining ingredients. Cover and reduce heat to simmer. Cook 30-45 minutes.

The longer it simmers, the richer the flavor and texture.

Downtime

dBASIC Sauce

Makes about 1 cup

2 tablespoons butter or margarine	1 cup milk
2 tablespoons all-purpose flour	Salt to taste

In heavy saucepan, melt butter over low heat. Stir in flour until smooth. Gradually add milk, stirring to keep sauce smooth. Cook and stir over medium heat until thickened. Add salt to taste.

ALT: For a quick cheese sauce,
stir in 1/2 cup grated cheese until melted.

THUK!

Boot

Easy Hollan-OOS Sauce

Makes 1-1/2 cups

1/3	stick butter or margarine	2	tablespoons lemon juice, freshly squeezed
1/4	cup flour		Dash salt
3/4	cup milk		
1/2	cup mayonnaise		

In heavy saucepan, melt butter over low heat. Slowly stir in flour. Add milk, stirring constantly until thick. Remove from heat. Add mayonnaise, lemon juice and salt. Stir well.

F.A.T. Reducer: Use diet margarine, lowfat milk and lowfat mayonnaise.

Excel-Lentil Soup

Serves 4-6 users

3	tablespoons butter or margarine	1	cup red or yellow lentils
1/2	small yellow onion, chopped	4-5	cups water
5	cloves garlic, pressed	1	slice lemon
3	thin slices fresh ginger root, peeled and grated		Salt to taste
	Dash cayenne pepper	1/4	cup cilantro leaves, chopped
	Green chili pepper to taste, seeded and minced		

Heat 2 tablespoons butter in medium saucepan over low heat. Sauté onion, garlic, ginger, cayenne and green chili. Cover and cook for 5 minutes. Add lentils, 4 cups water and lemon slice. Season with salt.

Cook for 20-30 minutes until lentils have thickened. Add extra water for thinner texture. Remove lemon slice before serving. Stir in chopped cilantro and serve.

Gaz-Batch-O

Makes about 7 cups

1	28-ounce can undrained tomatoes, chopped	1/4	cup olive oil
3/4	cup green bell pepper, chopped	1	tablespoon paprika
1/2	cup onion, chopped	1	teaspoon salt
1/2	cup cucumber, diced		Black pepper, freshly ground
3	cloves garlic, pressed		Tabasco sauce or cayenne pepper to taste.
2	cups prepared onion bouillon broth		Chopped parsley or cilantro, optional
1/2	cup lemon juice	1/2	cup toasted croutons

Combine all ingredients except croutons. Chill for at least 2 hours before serving. Garnish with croutons.

Make a batch today!

I-Corn Cheesy Chowder

* * * * * * * * * *

Serves 4-6 users

1	large potato, peeled and diced	3	tablespoons flour
2	bay leaves	1-1/4	cups milk
2	teaspoons cumin	2	cups grated cheddar cheese
2	cups water	1	16-1/2-ounce can corn, drained
1	small yellow onion, chopped		Salt and pepper to taste
1	2-ounce jar diced pimientos		
3	tablespoons butter		

In large soup pot, cook potato, bay leaves and cumin in boiling water about 15 minutes. In separate pan, sauté onion and pimientos in butter until tender. Blend in flour. Remove from heat and gradually add milk, stirring constantly.

Stir milk mixture and corn into potato mixture. Simmer for 5 minutes. Remove bay leaves. Add cheese and stir until it melts. Season with salt and pepper.

F.A.T. Reducer: Use lowfat milk and lowfat cheddar cheese.

Chapter 4
Megs and Cheese

Baked Macro-ni Casserole

Serves 6 users

1	8-ounce package elbow macaroni	1	2-ounce jar diced pimientos
1	10-3/4-ounce can cream of mushroom soup	1	cup grated cheddar cheese
		1/4	cup milk

Cook macaroni according to package directions and drain. In large mixing bowl, place macaroni and remaining ingredients. Mix well.

Place mixture in greased 2-quart casserole. Bake at 400 degrees F for 15-20 minutes or in microwave on high for 6-8 minutes. Remove and stir thoroughly before serving.

F.A.T. Reducer: Use lowfat cheddar cheese.

Egg Fried Mac-Rice

Serves 6 users

3	tablespoons vegetable or peanut oil	3	cups cooked rice, cold
1	cup chopped green onion and stem	2	tablespoons tamari or dark soy sauce
2	eggs, beaten	1/2	teaspoon ground white pepper, optional

Heat oil in wok or large frying pan. When hot, add onion and eggs. Stir quickly. Immediately add the rice, pressing it to the sides and bottom to separate. Stir in tamari or soy sauce and pepper, if desired. Serve topped with stir-fried vegetables.

Great way to use leftover rice.

Floppy Flapjacks

Serves 4-6 users

3	eggs	1/2	cup milk
1/2	cup flour	2	tablespoons oil
1/2	teaspoon salt		Butter or oil for frying

Beat eggs slightly. Add flour and salt. Stir until batter is smooth. Combine milk and oil. Stir into egg mixture until batter looks like heavy cream.

Heat small amount of butter or oil on griddle or skillet over medium-high heat. For each pancake, pour about 1/4 cup batter. Turn only once. Serve as pancakes or fill with ricotta or cottage cheese and fresh fruit or preserves.

De-bug

C'mon, Northern "nerds" — give it a try!

● ● ● ● ● ●

Hack Jack Cheese Grits

● ● ● ● ● ● ● ● ● ●

Serves 6 users

1	cup uncooked quick grits	1-1/2	cups Jack cheese, grated
4	cups water	1/3	cup butter or margarine
1-1/2	teaspoons salt	2	cloves garlic, crushed
2	eggs, beaten		Dash of hot sauce

Boot oven to 350 degrees F. Bring salted water to boil in medium saucepan. Slowly stir in grits. Cover, reduce heat and cook about 5 minutes, stirring occasionally until liquid is absorbed. Remove from heat.

Stir in remaining ingredients, mixing well. Pour mixture into greased 2-quart casserole. Bake for 30-40 minutes depending on depth of dish.

F.A.T. Reducer: Use lowfat cheese and diet margarine.

ALT: Add minced onion, diced green peppers, chopped mushrooms or other favorites.

55

Cut and Paste

Quick 'N' Quiche

* * * * * * * * * *

Makes 2 pies

1	tablespoon butter or margarine		Salt and pepper to taste
1	10-ounce package frozen chopped spinach, cooked and drained		Dash nutmeg
		1/2	pound grated Swiss cheese
		3/4	cup grated Parmesan cheese, divided
1	medium onion, diced		
4	eggs	2	9-inch no-lard pie crusts, unbaked
1	13-ounce can evaporated milk		

In frying pan, melt butter. Sauté drained spinach and onion. Set aside. In large mixing bowl, beat eggs, milk, salt, pepper and nutmeg until creamy. Stir in spinach mixture, Swiss cheese and 1/4 cup Parmesan cheese.

Pour equal amounts into pie crusts. Sprinkle the remaining Parmesan cheese on top. Bake at 350 degrees F for 40-45 minutes.

F.A.T. Reducer: Use evaporated skim milk and lowfat Swiss cheese. Skip the 1/4 cup Parmesan cheese topping.

Zu-Key-ni Pie

Makes 2 pies

2	zucchini squash, thinly sliced
1	tomato, peeled and chopped
1/2	red bell pepper, chopped
1/2	medium yellow onion, chopped
1	tablespoon olive oil
2	eggs

1-1/2	cups shredded Swiss cheese
1-1/2	cups shredded mozzarella cheese
2	cups bottled spaghetti sauce
2	9-inch no-lard pie crusts, prebaked for 10 minutes

Boot oven to 350 degrees F. In large pan, cook squash, tomatoes, bell pepper and onion in oil just until tender. Do not overcook vegetables. Beat eggs in large bowl. Add cheeses and stir.

Into each pie crust, layer equal amounts of vegetable mixture, spaghetti sauce and cheese mixture. Bake for 30-40 minutes.

F.A.T. Reducer: Use lowfat cheeses.

This is one time it's OK to freeze!

Chapter 5
Cut and Pasta

Angel Share Pasta

Serves 6 users

3	tablespoons olive oil
1/4	cup chopped green onions
2	cloves garlic, pressed
1/2	cup sun-dried tomatoes, chopped
1	14-1/2-ounce can tomatoes, drained (juice reserved) and chopped
1	bunch fresh basil leaves, chopped OR
1	tablespoon dried basil

Salt to taste

Freshly ground pepper, to taste

8 ounces fresh or dry angel hair pasta, cooked and drained

Grated Parmesan cheese

Heat oil in large skillet over low heat. Sauté green onions, garlic and sun-dried tomatoes for 1 minute. Add canned tomatoes, basil, salt and pepper. Simmer about 5 minutes until tomatoes are tender. If desired, add small amount of reserved tomato juice. Remove from heat.

Prepare pasta according to package directions and drain. Toss sauce with hot pasta and serve immediately. Sprinkle each serving with Parmesan cheese and freshly ground pepper.

ALT: For a gourmet touch, add 1 cup chopped marinated artichoke hearts when you add the canned tomatoes.

F.A.T. Reducer: Substitute diet margarine for olive oil.

Command-icotti

1   8-ounce package manicotti shells

1   32-ounce jar extra thick spaghetti sauce, divided

2   cups mozzarella cheese, shredded and divided

1   16-ounce carton ricotta cheese

12   2-inch saltine crackers, crushed

2   eggs, beaten

1/4 cup chives, chopped

1/2 teaspoon dried basil

1/2 teaspoon dried marjoram

1/4 teaspoon garlic salt

Cook shells and drain. Pour half of spaghetti sauce into lightly greased 9x13-inch baking dish. In large bowl, combine 1-1/2 cups mozzarella and remaining ingredients. Mix well. Stuff shells and arrange in prepared dish over sauce.

Pour remaining sauce over manicotti, and bake at 350 degrees F for 25 minutes. Sprinkle with remaining 1/2 cup mozzarella.

I SAID WORK!!

Command

61

Compress-to Pesto

Makes about 3 cups

2	cups fresh basil leaves	1	cup Parmesan cheese, grated
4	medium cloves garlic, chopped		Salt and freshly ground black pepper, to taste
1	cup walnuts or pine nuts		
1	cup olive oil		

Process the basil, garlic and walnuts or pine nuts in food processor or blender. With machine running, add oil in steady stream. Add cheese, pinch of salt and pepper to taste. Blend briefly to combine. Place in bowl and cover until ready to use. Store in refrigerator.

Serve over hot, fresh pasta.

ALT: Blend in 4 ounces cream cheese for a really creamy pesto.

F.A.T. Reducer: Access denied.

Disketti Spaghetti Sauce

Makes about 2 cups

1	medium yellow onion, diced	2-3	cups tomato sauce
3	cloves garlic, minced	1	teaspoon salt
2	tablespoons oil	1	teaspoon dried basil
1	cup bulghur (cracked) wheat	1/2	teaspoon oregano

In large skillet, sauté onion and garlic in oil over low heat until onion is translucent. Add bulghur. Sauté briefly, stirring to coat well. Stir in 2 cups sauce, salt and spices. Cover and let simmer, stirring occasionally. Cook for 10-15 minutes until mixture is slightly chewy, adding more sauce if necessary.

Use in any recipe needing spaghetti sauce for hearty, lowfat fare.

Fett-Icon-E Alfredo

Serves 6 users

1	8-ounce package fettucine	2	tablespoons butter or margarine, melted
1/3	cup milk	1/2	cup grated Parmesan cheese, divided
1	cup ricotta or cottage cheese		Dash nutmeg, optional
1	egg yolk		
1/4	teaspoon freshly ground black pepper		

Cook fettucine according to package directions. Drain and set aside. In food processor or blender, blend milk, cottage cheese, egg and pepper. In saucepan, melt butter over low heat. Add cheese mixture and bring to a simmer, stirring occasionally.

Stir in all but 6 teaspoons Parmesan cheese. Pour mixture over fettucine and toss. Sprinkle each serving with remaining Parmesan cheese and dash nutmeg, if desired.

F.A.T. Reducer: Use lowfat milk, lowfat cottage cheese and diet margarine.

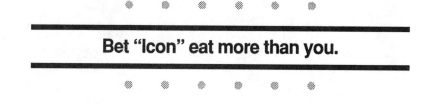

Bet "Icon" eat more than you.

Root

* * * * * *

Computer nuts will pine for this one.

---

* * * * * *

Font-u-cine with Pine Nuts

* * * * * * * * * *

Serves 6 users

4	tablespoons butter or margarine		1	medium clove garlic, pressed
1/2	cup pine nuts		1	tablespoon chopped parsley
1/2	cup seasoned bread crumbs		1	8-ounce package fettucine

Melt butter in small pan over low heat. Add pine nuts, bread crumbs and garlic. Stir frequently until nuts and crumbs are golden brown. Stir in parsley and cook for 30 seconds. Remove from heat.

Cook noodles according to package directions. Drain and place in serving bowl. Pour nut mixture over fettucine and toss gently.

Link-guine Stroganoff

Serves 6 users

3	tablespoons butter or margarine	1	tablespoon tamari or soy sauce, optional
3	cups sliced mushrooms		Dash paprika
2	cups sour cream	1	8-ounce package linguine, cooked and drained
1	envelope dry onion bouillon		
1	teaspoon garlic powder		

Heat butter in large skillet. Sauté mushrooms. Place sour cream in mixing bowl. Stir in bouillon, garlic powder and tamari, if desired. Mix thoroughly.

When mushrooms are soft, pour sour cream mixture into skillet. Stir to mix. Let mixture heat slightly. Toss over noodles and sprinkle with paprika.

F.A.T. Reducer: Use lowfat sour cream.

You'll lap link this up!

∏oodles ROⅢ-ano

* * * * * * * * * * *

Serves 6 users

1/4	cup butter or margarine		Salt and freshly ground pepper
1/2	teaspoon grated nutmeg		
2/3	cup heavy cream or half-and-half	2	cups grated Parmesan cheese, divided
1	12-ounce package fettucine cooked and drained		

Melt butter in large saucepan. Add nutmeg and half the cream. Stir until bubbles start to appear. Add the fettucine and stir to coat. Pour in remaining cream and 1 cup cheese alternately, stirring pasta to mix. Salt and pepper to taste. Sprinkle each serving with remaining Parmesan.

F.A.T. Reducer: Make "Fett-Icon-E Alfredo" instead.

PC Shells

Serves 6 users

3	cups ricotta cheese	1	teaspoon garlic powder
1/2	cup grated Parmesan cheese	1	12-ounce package jumbo shells, cooked and drained
1	egg	3-4	cups spaghetti sauce
1/4	teaspoon salt	1	cup grated Parmesan
1/2	teaspoon black pepper		cheese for top

Combine ricotta, Parmesan cheese, egg, salt, pepper and garlic powder in bowl. Stuff shells. Cover bottom of baking dish with 1 cup spaghetti sauce. Arrange stuffed shells in dish and pour remaining spaghetti sauce over all.

Cover and bake 25 minutes at 350 degrees F. Uncover and sprinkle with Parmesan cheese. Bake an additional five minutes.

ALT: Add 1 cup cooked and drained chopped spinach to filling. Continue as above.

F.A.T. Reducer: Use skim milk ricotta cheese.

You'll C: prompt smiles when you serve this.

Prompt Primavera

Serves 4-6 users

1	16-ounce bag frozen Italian style vegetables	1	16-ounce package spaghetti, cooked and drained
2	tablespoons cornstarch		
2	envelopes dry vegetable bouillon *	1	cup grated Parmesan cheese
1-1/2	cups water		

Steam or microwave vegetables until crisp-tender. Keep covered and set aside. In saucepan over medium heat, combine cornstarch and dry bouillon with 1/4 cup water. Stir until cornstarch dissolves. Add remaining water and bring to boil. Reduce heat, stirring constantly until thickened.

In large serving bowl, toss vegetables, sauce, pasta and Parmesan cheese. Mix thoroughly and serve "promptly".

* Available in the soup, health food or kosher section of most grocery stores.

Spicy Sesame CO Noodles

● ● ● ● ● ● ● ● ● ●

Serves 4-6 users

2	tablespoons sesame oil	1/8	teaspoon cayenne pepper or to taste
3	tablespoons tahini (sesame paste)	3	teaspoons brown sugar
2	tablespoons peanut butter	2	teaspoons rice vinegar
2	tablespoons tamari or soy sauce	3	tablespoons green onion tops, thinly sliced
2	cloves garlic, pressed	1	8-ounce package spaghetti, cooked, drained and cooled
1/4	teaspoon fresh ginger root, minced		

In food processor or blender, blend all ingredients except 1 tablespoon green onions and spaghetti. Blend until creamy. Thin with small amount of water if too thick.

Toss over spaghetti and garnish with remaining green onions.

Chapter 6
Sidekicks

ASCII Asparagus

Serves 4-6 users

1	pound fresh asparagus		1	teaspoon salt
2	tablespoons oil		1	teaspoon sugar

Wash asparagus in cold water. Remove tough stem ends. Cut tender parts into 1-inch diamond-shaped pieces by making a diagonal slice, rolling half a turn and slicing again.

Heat oil in very hot skillet or wok. Add asparagus when oil starts smoking. Stir-fry until each piece is coated. Add salt and sugar and stir for 1-2 minutes. Serve hot or cold.

Top with "Easy Hollan-DOS Sauce".

Scanner

Optimize your disk while chopping.

Data-touille

Makes about 4 cups

2	tablespoons olive oil	1	medium zucchini, chopped
1	medium onion, chopped	3	cloves garlic, minced
1	28-ounce can undrained tomatoes, chopped	1/8	teaspoon basil and/or oregano
1	small green bell pepper, chopped		Salt and pepper to taste
1	medium eggplant, peeled and chopped	1	bay leaf

In large skillet, sauté onion in oil. Add remaining ingredients. Cook until tender, about 20 minutes. Remove bay leaf. Serve warm over rice or chill and serve as appetizer.

Disk Dumplings

Serves 4-6 users

6-8	cups prepared vegetable bouillon broth *	1	large egg, lightly beaten
1/2	cup grated Parmesan cheese	2	tablespoons fresh basil, parsley or cilantro, minced
1/2	cup ricotta cheese		Green onion tops, thinly sliced
1/2	cup all-purpose flour		

Heat broth until simmering in large pot. In medium bowl, stir the Parmesan cheese, ricotta, flour, egg, and herb of choice just until smooth. Scoop about 1 tablespoon mixture with rounded spoon and with second spoon, smooth top into a dumpling.

Drop into simmering soup and repeat until all dumplings are formed. Simmer until dumplings are cooked through, about 6 minutes. Serve in bowl with broth and top with green onion.

* Available in the soup, health food or kosher section of most grocery stores.

Mac 'n' Tosh Squash

Serves 6 users

3	medium zucchini, sliced	1/4	teaspoon ground black pepper
1/2	cup chopped onion		
2	tablespoons olive oil	2	tomatoes, peeled and sliced
16	ounces cottage cheese	1/2	cup grated Parmesan cheese
1	teaspoon basil		
1/2	teaspoon oregano		

Sauté zucchini and onion in oil until onion is translucent. In blender or mixer, whip cottage cheese with basil, oregano and pepper.

In 2-quart greased baking dish, alternate layers of zucchini, cottage cheese mixture and tomato slices. Top with Parmesan cheese. Bake at 350 degrees F for 25-30 minutes.

Even PC lovers will like this Mac.

Del Dill Potatoes

Serves 4 users

3   large white potatoes, peeled and chopped

1   green onion, finely chopped

1   teaspoon dried dill

4   tablespoons grated Parmesan cheese

Steam or microwave potatoes until tender. Blend in food processor or blender until smooth. Stir in onion and dill. Spread on greased baking sheet. Sprinkle with cheese and bake at 400 degrees F until browned, about 10-15 minutes.

Marsh-Mono Sweet Potatoes

Serves 6 users

4-5   large sweet potatoes

3   tablespoons butter or margarine, melted

4   tablespoons brown sugar

1/2   teaspoon cinnamon

1   7-ounce jar marshmallow creme

Bake sweet potatoes at 350 degrees F for about 30 minutes or microwave on high for about 12 minutes. Let cool and peel off skin. Mash in medium bowl. Stir in butter, brown sugar and cinnamon. Heat through.

Place mixture in 2-quart greased baking dish and spread top with marshmallow creme. Place in broiler and broil about 4 inches from flame until top is golden.

Shish CO-BOLs

8	ounces firm tofu	**Marinade:**	
2	cups cubed vegetables/ fruits (onion, zucchini, bell pepper,eggplant, pineapple, whole cherry tomatoes)	2	tablespoons garlic, minced
		1	teaspoon onion powder
		1/4	teaspoon ground oregano
	Olive oil	1	tablespoon soy sauce or tamari
		2	tablespoons rice vinegar or lemon juice

Mix marinade ingredients in bowl. Place tofu on large plate lined with paper towels and cover with paper towels. Top with large plate. Let drain for 10 minutes. Cut tofu into 2-inch cubes. Place in marinade for 30 minutes, turning frequently.

Preheat broiler or grill. Alternate tofu, vegetables and fruit on skewers. Brush all lightly with olive oil. Broil or grill until lightly browned. Serve hot.

Watch how fast you pick up this language.

Spanish Mac-Rice

* * * * * * * * * *

Serves 6 users

1	yellow onion, diced	2	cups tomato sauce
2	cloves garlic, minced	1	teaspoon salt
1	cup chopped green bell pepper	1	teaspoon paprika
2	tablespoons olive oil	1/2	teaspoon black pepper
3	cups cooked rice (quick-cooking type OK)		Dash cayenne pepper

In large skillet, sauté onion, garlic and bell pepper in oil over low heat until onion is translucent. Add rice and sauté briefly. Stir in tomato sauce and spices. Heat through and serve.

Ci-LAN-tro Rice

* * * * * * * * * *

Serves 6 users

3	tablespoons butter or margarine		Pepper to taste
1	cup white rice	2	cups water
1	tablespoon dry vegetable bouillon *	1/2	cup toasted pine nuts or slivered almonds
1/2	cup fresh cilantro leaves, chopped		

Melt butter in medium saucepan. Add rice and stir to coat. Stir in bouillon, cilantro, pepper and water. Bring water to boil. Reduce heat to simmer and cover.

Cook rice according to package directions, adding more water if necessary. When rice is done, stir in nuts. Serve immediately.

* Available in the soup, health food or kosher section of most grocery stores.

Using Windows Efficiently

Stir-Fried Block-oli

Serves 4-6 users

1	pound broccoli, rinsed in cold water	1/4	teaspoon sugar
1/4	cup vegetable or peanut oil	3	tablespoons soy sauce or tamari
1	clove garlic, crushed	1/4	cup water
1/2	teaspoon salt		
1	teaspoon rice wine or dry sherry		

Cut broccoli into 2-inch flowerets and slice stems 1/4-inch thick. Heat oil in wok or large skillet over high heat for 30 seconds. Stir-fry garlic for 30 seconds. Add stems and salt. Stir-fry 30 seconds. Add flowerets and stir-fry 1 minute.

Add wine, sugar, soy sauce and water. Reduce heat to medium low and stir-fry until water is almost gone. Serve immediately.

Select this "block-oli" and move to your tummy.

Using Windows Efficiently

Stir-Fried Block-oli

Serves 4-6 users

1	pound broccoli, rinsed in cold water	1/4	teaspoon sugar
1/4	cup vegetable or peanut oil	3	tablespoons soy sauce or tamari
1	clove garlic, crushed	1/4	cup water
1/2	teaspoon salt		
1	teaspoon rice wine or dry sherry		

Cut broccoli into 2-inch flowerets and slice stems 1/4-inch thick. Heat oil in wok or large skillet over high heat for 30 seconds. Stir-fry garlic for 30 seconds. Add stems and salt. Stir-fry 30 seconds. Add flowerets and stir-fry 1 minute.

Add wine, sugar, soy sauce and water. Reduce heat to medium low and stir-fry until water is almost gone. Serve immediately.

Select this "block-oli" and move to your tummy.

Chapter 7
Mainframe
Dishes

Hacker Helper

Makes about 2 cups

1	medium yellow onion, diced	1	cup bulghur (cracked) wheat
3	cloves garlic, minced	2-3	cups water
2	tablespoons oil	1	teaspoon salt

In large skillet, sauté onion and garlic in oil over low heat until onion is translucent. Add bulghur. Sauté briefly, stirring to coat well. Stir in 2 cups water and salt. Cover and let simmer, stirring occasionally. Cook for 10-15 minutes until mixture is slightly chewy, adding more water if necessary.

Hacker

**Freeze a batch of "Hacker Helper"
and keep on hand for the following dishes.**

Enchil-Load-DOS

Makes 10-12 enchiladas

1	recipe "Hacker Helper"	10-12 medium-sized soft flour tortillas
2	teaspoons cumin	
1	teaspoon chili powder	1-1/2 cups Jack or cheddar cheese, grated
1/4	teaspoon cayenne pepper or to taste	Chopped cilantro leaves for garnish
2	cups prepared salsa, divided	

In large skillet, prepare or reheat "Hacker Helper". Stir in spices and 1/2 cup salsa. Simmer until heated through.

Fill tortillas one at a time with 2-3 tablespoons wheat mixture and sprinkle with 2 tablespoons cheese. Roll up and place seam side down into a large shallow baking dish. Top with remaining salsa and cheese. Bake at 350 degrees F for 20 minutes. Garnish with cilantro.

F.A.T. Reducer: Use lowfat cheese.

Ta-CO-BOL Tacos

Makes 10-12 tacos

1	recipe "Hacker Helper"	**Fillings:**
3	tablespoons taco seasoning mix	Sour cream, chopped tomatoes, grated cheddar cheese, avocado, cilantro, black olives
1/2	cup bottled salsa	
10-12	taco shells	

In large skillet, prepare or reheat "Hacker Helper". Stir in spices and salsa. Simmer until heated through.

Boot oven to 350 degrees F. Line up taco shells on baking sheet. Place 2-3 tablespoons filling in each and bake for 5-7 minutes. Remove from oven and top with optional fillings above.

F.A.T. Reducer: Skip the cheese and sour cream as toppings or use lowfat versions.

Turbo-ritos

* * * * * * * * * *

Makes 10-12 burritos

1   recipe "Hacker Helper"

3   tablespoons taco seasoning
      mix

1   16-ounce can no-lard refried
      beans, heated through

10-12 medium-sized flour tortillas

Fillings:

Sour cream, chopped
jalapeños, black olives,
tomatoes

In large skillet, prepare or reheat "Hacker Helper". Stir in taco seasoning. Simmer until heated through.

Heat tortillas according to package directions. To make burritos, spread 1/4 cup wheat mixture, 1/4 cup refried beans and 3 tablespoons of optional fillings in center of tortilla. Fold bottom of tortilla up slightly, then fold sides to meet in center.

* * * * *

They'll disappear at turbo speed!

* * * * *

Binary Beanery Chili

Serves 6-8 users

2	tablespoons olive oil		1	cup tomato sauce
1	medium onion, chopped		1	medium green bell pepper, chopped
3	medium garlic cloves, pressed		2	15-ounce cans pinto or kidney beans, drained
1-1/2	tablespoons cumin			Salt and black pepper to taste
	Chili powder to taste			
1	cup bulghur (cracked) wheat			
1	28-ounce can undrained tomatoes, coarsely chopped			

In large skillet, sauté onion, garlic, cumin and chili powder in oil over low heat until onion is translucent. Add bulghur. Sauté briefly, stirring to coat. Add remaining ingredients. Let simmer for 30-45 minutes, stirring occasionally.

F.A.T. Reducer: Sauté onion and garlic in water.

There'll be nary a bowl left.

Lowfat Laser-gna

Serves 12 users

2   cups lowfat ricotta cheese

1   cup lowfat cottage cheese

1   tablespoon dried basil

1   tablespoon dried parsley

1   teaspoon garlic powder

4   cups bottled spaghetti
    sauce

1   cup grated part skim
    mozzarella cheese

3/4 pound uncooked lasagna
    noodles

1/2 cup grated Parmesan
    cheese

Boot oven to 350 degrees F. In large bowl, combine first 5 ingredients. Pour 1 cup spaghetti sauce in bottom of greased 9x13-inch baking dish. Arrange 1 layer of noodles over sauce. Top with 1/2 of the ricotta mixture and sprinkle with 1/2 cup mozzarella cheese.

Continue layering with 1 cup spaghetti sauce, 1 layer noodles, remaining ricotta mixture and rest of the mozzarella cheese. Add another cup of sauce, layer of noodles and remaining sauce. Sprinkle with Parmesan cheese. Cover tightly with lid or aluminum foil. Bake for one hour.

The noodles cook while baking.

Mex-Icon Corn Casserole

Serves 6-8 users

3	cups cooked rice (quick-cooking type OK)	1	4-ounce can mild green chilies, drained
2	cups sour cream	1	cup shredded Jack cheese
5	green onions, chopped	1/4	cup shredded cheddar cheese
	Salt and pepper to taste		
1	14-1/2-ounce can corn, drained	3	tablespoons chopped fresh cilantro

Boot oven to 350 degrees F. In large bowl, mix rice and sour cream. Stir in green onions, salt and pepper. Spread 1/2 rice mixture in bottom of greased 2-quart casserole. Top with half the corn, half the chilies and half the Jack cheese.

Repeat with remaining rice, corn, chilies and Jack cheese. Top with cheddar cheese. Bake uncovered for 20 minutes, uncovered for 10 more minutes. Sprinkle with cilantro and serve.

F.A.T. Reducer: Use light sour cream and lowfat cheese.

PC-Rice Mexi-Casserole

● ● ● ● ● ● ● ● ● ●

Serves 6 users

2	cups cooked rice (quick-cooking type OK)	1/2	cup bottled taco sauce
2	tablespoons butter or margarine	2	cups shredded cheddar cheese
3	tablespoons taco seasoning mix	12	large tortilla chips, crushed
1	16-ounce can no-lard refried beans	1-2	cups sour cream
			Sliced black olives

In medium bowl, combine rice, butter and taco seasonings. In separate bowl, combine refried beans and 1/3 cup taco sauce. Spread half of bean mixture in bottom of 2-quart casserole. Top with half the rice mixture, 1/4 cup taco sauce, 1 cup cheese and chips. Repeat layers, excluding chips.

Bake at 350 degrees F for 20 minutes. Remove from oven and top with sour cream and olives. Bake again for 5 minutes.

F.A.T. Reducer: Use lowfat cheese and lowfat sour cream.

Greek Mouse-saka

Serves 6-8 users

1	large eggplant, peeled
2	cups cooked rice (quick-cooking type OK)
2	cups bottled spaghetti sauce
1/2	cup chopped parsley or cilantro
	Pinch cinnamon
	Salt and pepper to taste

1	10-3/4-ounce can cream of mushroom soup
1	15-ounce carton ricotta cheese
1/2	cup milk
	Nutmeg to taste
	Grated Parmesan cheese
	Seasoned bread crumbs

Cut eggplant into thin slices. To remove bitterness, salt lightly on each side and place on paper towels. In large bowl, stir together cooked rice, spaghetti sauce, parsley or cilantro, cinnamon, salt and pepper. In food processor or blender, mix cream of mushroom soup, ricotta cheese, milk and nutmeg.

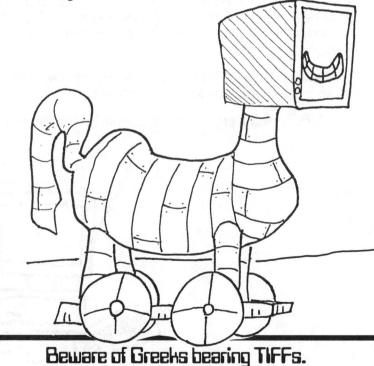

Beware of Greeks bearing TIFFs.

Boot oven to 375 degrees F. Grease a 3-quart baking dish and sprinkle bottom lightly with bread crumbs. Alternate layers of eggplant and rice mixture, sprinkling each layer generously with Parmesan cheese and bread crumbs.

Pour soup mixture over top of casserole and bake 1 hour or until top is golden.

F.A.T. Reducer: Use skim milk ricotta cheese and lowfat milk.

Middle Eastern Fela-File

Serves 6 users

3	slices firm whole wheat bread, crustless	2	tablespoons chopped parsley
2	tablespoons fresh lemon juice	1/4	teaspoon salt
		1/4	teaspoon black pepper
2	tablespoons all-purpose flour	1/2	teaspoon ground cumin
		1/4	teaspoon basil
2	tablespoons tahini (sesame paste) or olive oil	1	15-ounce can chickpeas, drained
3	garlic cloves, pressed		Cayenne pepper to taste
1	egg		Oil or margarine for frying

In blender or food processor, blend all ingredients except chickpeas until smooth. Add chickpeas and blend only to a rough consistency — not too smooth. Add cayenne pepper to taste.

Heat 1-2 tablespoons of oil or margarine in skillet or griddle. Pour 1/3 cup mixture on skillet for each pattie. Brown each side. Serve with plain yogurt.

Turbo Tofu Burgers

* * * * * * * * * *

Makes 6 burgers

1	pound firm tofu, drained and mashed	2	teaspoons tamari or soy sauce
1	envelope dry onion soup mix	3	tablespoons toasted sesame seeds
1	teaspoon garlic powder	2-3	cups seasoned stuffing mix
2	eggs, beaten		Butter or oil for frying

Combine all ingredients except stuffing in large bowl. Mix thoroughly with hands. Mix in stuffing until texture is firm enough to form patties. Let sit for five minutes. Using about 2/3 cup of the mixture per ball, flatten into patties.

Heat small amount of oil or butter in pan or skillet. Fry patties until brown or crispy on both sides.

UGA Ueggie Chili

● ● ● ● ● ● ● ● ● ●

Serves 8-10 users

3	tablespoons olive oil			Jalapeño pepper to taste, seeded and minced
1	large onion, chopped		2	15-ounce cans black beans, drained
5	medium garlic cloves, pressed			
3	tablespoons cumin		1/2	cup chopped cilantro leaves
2	cups chopped zucchini		3	tablespoons fresh lime juice
1	28-ounce can undrained tomatoes, coarsely chopped			Salt and black pepper to taste
1	medium red bell pepper, seeded and chopped			

In large pot, heat oil over low heat. Sauté onion, garlic and cumin until onion is translucent. Add zucchini, tomatoes, bell and jalapeño peppers, beans and cilantro. Cover and let simmer for 45 minutes, stirring occasionally. Just before serving, stir in lime juice, salt and black pepper.

F.A.T. Reducer: Sauté onion and garlic in water.

Click

Chapter 8
Breads and Scrolls

B-RAM Muffins

* * * * * * * * * *

Makes 15-18 muffins

1	cup pure maple syrup or honey	1	cup all-purpose flour
2	eggs	1	cup wheat bran
1	cup sour cream	1	teaspoon baking soda
2	tablespoons oil	1	cup raisins

Boot oven to 350 degrees F. In large mixing bowl or food processor, mix all ingredients except raisins. Fold in raisins. Fill greased muffin tins 2/3 full with batter. Bake for 15-20 minutes until top bounces back when touched.

F.A.T. Reducer: Use lowfat sour cream.

* * * * * *

Don't RAM them all in your mouth at once!

---

* * * * * *

Ba-Nano Nut Bread

Makes 2 loaves

6	ripe bananas, peeled	1	teaspoon baking soda
1	stick butter or margarine, melted	1	teaspoon salt
		4	cups all-purpose flour
2	eggs	1	cup chopped nuts
1-1/2	cups sugar OR 1 cup honey		

Boot oven to 325 degrees F. Grease 2 9x5-inch loaf pans. In large mixing bowl or food processor, mix first 3 ingredients. Slowly blend in sugar or honey.

In separate bowl, combine baking soda, salt and flour. Merge wet and dry ingredients. Stir in nuts. Pour even amounts in loaf pans. Bake for 40-50 minutes until toothpick or fork inserted in center of loaf comes out clean.

Path

Ched-Oir Corn Br-Ed

Serves 8-12 users

1-1/2	cups yellow cornmeal	2	eggs
1/2	cup unbleached white flour	1-1/2	cups buttermilk or plain yogurt
1/2	teaspoon salt		
	Cumin, chili powder and/or cayenne pepper to taste	1	cup cheddar cheese, shredded
2	teaspoons baking powder		**Options:**
3	tablespoons melted butter or oil		Sliced green chilies, diced jalapeños, sweet red peppers, minced onions
2	tablespoons honey		

Boot oven to 400 degrees F. Combine dry ingredients in medium bowl. In blender or food processor, blend liquid ingredients until creamy. Stir in cheese and optional ingredients.

Merge wet and dry mixtures. Do not overmix. Pour into a greased 8x8-inch baking pan. Bake for 35-40 minutes. Cool on a wire rack.

Low Density Biskettes

2	cups all-purpose flour	3	tablespoons butter or margarine
1	teaspoon baking powder		
1/2	teaspoon salt	1/2	cup milk or buttermilk

Boot oven to 400 degrees F. Combine the first 3 ingredients in a large bowl. Mix thoroughly. Cut the butter into the flour mixture with a fork. Stir in the milk and mix well. Knead dough for a few minutes.

Roll out on floured surface to about 3/4-inch thickness. Cut out biscuits with a cutter and place on a greased baking sheet. Bake until lightly browned on top.

Mother Board

Pineapple Zoom-chini Bread

* * * * * * * * * *

Makes 2 loaves

3	cups unbleached white flour	3	eggs
1	teaspoon baking soda	3/4	cup oil
1/2	teaspoon baking powder	1	teaspoon vanilla
1	teaspoon nutmeg	1	cup chopped walnuts
2	teaspoons cinnamon	1	20-ounce can crushed
1	teaspoon salt		pineapple, drained
2	cups brown sugar, packed		
2	cups finely-shredded zucchini		

Sub-directory

Boot oven to 350 degrees F. Mix first 7 ingredients in large bowl. In separate bowl, beat zucchini, eggs, oil and vanilla until creamy. Merge wet and dry ingredients thoroughly. Fold in nuts and pineapple.

Pour batter into 2 greased 9x5-inch loaf pans. Bake for 60-70 minutes. Bread is done when toothpick or fork inserted in center comes out clean. Cool in pan for 10 minutes, remove and cool thoroughly on wire rack.

Pumpkin Rais-Input Nut Bread

Makes 2 loaves

3	cups all-purpose flour		4	eggs
3	cups sugar		1	cup oil
2	teaspoons baking soda		1/3	cup water
1	teaspoon nutmeg		1	teaspoon vanilla
2	teaspoons cinnamon		1	cup chopped pecans or walnuts
1	teaspoon salt			
1	16-ounce can pumpkin		1	cup raisins

Boot oven to 350 degrees F. Mix first 6 ingredients in large bowl. In separate bowl, beat pumpkin, eggs, oil, water and vanilla. Merge wet and dry ingredients. Stir in nuts and raisins.

Pour into 2 greased 9x5-inch loaf pans. Bake for 60-70 minutes. Cool in pan for 10 minutes. Remove and cool thoroughly on wire rack.

Better not input all of this by yourself.

Quick Cheese Scrolls

Makes 12 rolls

6	bake and serve rolls		1/4	cup Parmesan cheese
1/4	cup butter or margarine, melted		2	egg whites, beaten
1/2	cup grated cheddar cheese, room temperature			

Boot oven to 350 degrees F. Cut rolls in half, crossways. Mix butter, cheddar and Parmesan cheese, onion and egg whites. Spread mixture on rolls. Bake for 10-15 minutes until golden brown.

Chapter 9
Appli-Cake-Tions

Apple-DOS Cake

Serves 24-36 users

1	stick butter or margarine, softened	2-1/2	cups flour
1-1/2	cups sugar	1-1/2	teaspoons baking soda
2	eggs	1/2	teaspoon salt
2	cups applesauce	1	teaspoon cinnamon
		1	cup butterscotch chips

Boot oven to 350 degrees F. Beat margarine and sugar until creamy. Beat in eggs and applesauce. In separate bowl, combine flour, baking soda, salt and cinnamon. Merge dry and wet ingredients, mixing well. Pour batter into greased 9x13-inch baking pan. Sprinkle butterscotch chips evenly over top.

Bake for 2 minutes. Remove and swirl chips through batter with a knife. Return to oven and bake for 30 minutes. Cool in pan on wire rack. Cut into bars.

You'll be the apple of someone's I/O when you make this.

Apple II Cake

Serves 6 users

2	cups diced, peeled apples	1	cup all-purpose flour
1	cup sugar	1	teaspoon baking soda
1/4	cup oil	1	teaspoon cinnamon
1	egg, beaten	1/4	teaspoon salt
1	teaspoon vanilla	1/2	cup chopped nuts, optional

Toss apples and sugar together in medium bowl. Stir in oil, egg and vanilla. In separate bowl, combine flour, baking soda, cinnamon and salt. Merge wet and dry mixtures. Stir in nuts, if desired.

Boot oven to 350 degrees F. Pour batter into a 9x5-inch loaf pan. Bake for 25-30 minutes.

ALT: Replace apples with 2 cups diced zucchini for a unique treat.

* * * * * *

Insert this floppy and enjoy!
---

* * * * * *

Cinnamon "Floppy"

* * * * * * * * * *

Serves 4-6 users

1	cup sugar	3/4	cup milk
1-1/4	cups flour	1/3	cup brown sugar
2	teaspoons baking powder	1/2	teaspoon cinnamon
3	tablespoons butter or margarine, divided		

Boot oven to 350 degrees F. In mixing bowl, stir together first three ingredients. Cut in 1 tablespoon butter. Add milk. Mix all together. Pour into greased pie pan. Sprinkle brown sugar and cinnamon on top. Dot with remaining butter. Bake 30 minutes.

Disk Doubler

Cinna-Mono Crumb Coffee Cake

Serves 24 users

Batter:

1	box yellow cake mix
3	eggs
2/3	cup water
1	stick butter or margarine

Crumbs:

1	cup sugar
3	cups flour
3	sticks butter or margarine, softened
1	tablespoon cinnamon
	Pinch salt
	Powdered sugar for dusting top

Boot oven to 350 degrees F. In large mixing bowl, beat batter ingredients until mixed. Pour into a well-greased 9x13-inch baking pan. Bake for 20 minutes.

Mix all crumb ingredients except powdered sugar until crumbly. Sprinkle over cake and bake for 20 more minutes. Remove and sprinkle with powdered sugar. Let cool.

Cut And Taste Coffee Cake

* * * * * * * * * *

Serves 24 users

4	large cans refrigerator biscuits	1/2	cup chopped pecans, optional
1	cup sugar	3/4	cup brown sugar
1-1/2	tablespoons cinnamon	3	sticks butter or margarine
1/2	cup raisins		

Boot oven to 350 degrees F. Cut each biscuit into 4 pieces. Mix sugar and cinnamon in plastic bag. Add biscuits and shake until coated. Arrange pieces in greased tube pan. Sprinkle with raisins and pecans, if desired.

In medium pan, boil brown sugar and butter. Pour over biscuits. Bake for 35-40 minutes. Cool.

Access Denied

This is one spreadsheet you'll love getting into.

Gooey Butter Spreadsheet Cake

Serves 24-36 users

1	box yellow butter cake mix		1	16-ounce package powdered sugar
2	eggs			
1	stick butter or margarine, melted		2	eggs
			1	teaspoon vanilla
1	8-ounce package cream cheese, softened			

Boot oven to 350 degrees F. In large mixing bowl or food processor, mix first 3 ingredients until smooth. Spread mixture into well-greased 9x13-inch baking pan. Mix remaining ingredients until creamy. Pour over cake batter.

Bake for 35-40 minutes, just until cake pulls away from sides. Cake will appear slightly sticky. Cool and cut into bars.

Mac Apple Torte

* * * * * * * * * *

Serves 6-8 users

Pastry:

1   *stick butter or margarine*
1/3 *cup sugar*
1/4 *teaspoon vanilla*
1   *cup flour*

Filling:

1   *8-ounce package cream cheese, softened*
1/4 *cup sugar*
1   *egg*
1/2 *teaspoon vanilla*

Fruit layer:

1   *21-ounce can apple pie filling*

Topping:

1/2 *cup sour cream*
1   *tablespoon sugar*
      Dash cinnamon

Boot oven to 450 degrees F. In mixing bowl, cream butter, sugar and vanilla. Blend in flour. Spread dough onto bottom and sides of 9-inch springform pan.

In same bowl, beat cream cheese, sugar, egg and vanilla until creamy. Pour into pastry-lined pan. Spoon apple pie filling over cream cheese layer.

Bake for 10 minutes. Reduce heat to 400 degrees F and bake 25 more minutes. Prepare topping by mixing sour cream and sugar. Remove torte from oven. Spread topping over apples and sprinkle lightly with cinnamon. Bake 5 more minutes. Cool before removing rim from pan.

* * * * * *

**A "bit" long, but Mac users
can make this with all that time
they think they save.**

---

* * * * * *

G-RAM Cracker Crust

Makes 1 9-inch pie crust

1-1/4 cups finely-ground graham cracker crumbs

2 tablespoons sugar

1/3 cup butter or margarine, melted

Combine crumbs and sugar. Add melted butter and mix well. With back of spoon, press firmly on bottom and sides of 9-inch pie pan. Bake at 300 degrees F for 5-8 minutes. Allow to cool before filling.

※   ※   ※   ※   ※   ※

They'll be no leftovers to account for.

※   ※   ※   ※   ※   ※

Peach-Tree Cheesecake

※   ※   ※   ※   ※   ※   ※   ※   ※   ※

Serves 12 users

1	9-inch graham cracker crust	1/3	cup fresh lemon juice
1	8-ounce package cream cheese, softened	1	teaspoon vanilla extract
1	14-ounce can sweetened condensed milk	1	21-ounce can peach pie filling, chilled

In large mixing bowl, beat cream cheese until fluffy. Gradually beat in sweetened condensed milk until smooth. Stir in lemon juice and vanilla. Pour into crust.

Chill until set, at least 4 hours. Top with pie filling before serving. Keep leftovers chilled (if there are any).

ALT: Top with other chilled fruit pie fillings before serving.

Pineapple Backup-Side Down Cake

* * * * * * * * * *

Serves 24-36 users

2	20-ounce cans juice-packed crushed pineapple	1/4	teaspoon nutmeg
1	cup honey, divided	1/2	teaspoon salt
1	cup whole wheat flour	1/2	cup vanilla yogurt
1	cup all-purpose flour	1/3	cup butter or margarine, melted
1	tablespoon baking powder	2	eggs
1	teaspoon cinnamon	2	teaspoons vanilla

Drain pineapple in a strainer and reserve juice. Mix pineapple and 1/2 cup honey. Pour mixture into a greased 8x8-inch glass baking dish. Boot oven to 350 degrees F.

Mix dry ingredients in large bowl. In separate bowl, mix 1/2 cup pineapple juice with remaining honey and rest of ingredients. Stir thoroughly. Merge wet and dry ingredients and mix well. Pour over the pineapple in baking pan.

Bake for 40-45 minutes or until a toothpick or fork inserted in center comes out clean. Cool for 20 minutes. Turn over onto a plate for serving.

* * * * * *

You'll be "backup" for more.

* * * * * *

Backup

Spicebar Cake

Serves 24-36 users

2	cups all-purpose flour
1-1/2	cups brown sugar, packed
1	teaspoons baking powder
1-1/4	teaspoons baking soda
2	teaspoons cinnamon
3/4	teaspoon ground cloves
1/2	teaspoon nutmeg
1/2	cup butter or margarine, softened
1/4	cup oil
2	eggs
1	cup sour cream
1	cup raisins
1/2	cup chopped walnuts

Icing:

1	8-ounce package cream cheese, softened
1	stick butter or margarine, softened
1	16-ounce box powdered sugar

Boot oven to 350 degrees F. In large bowl, mix first 7 ingredients. In separate bowl, beat butter, oil, eggs and sour cream until creamy. Stir in raisins and nuts. Merge wet and dry mixtures thoroughly.

Pour batter into a greased 9x13-inch baking pan. Bake for 40-45 minutes until a toothpick or fork comes out clean when inserted. Let cool.

To prepare icing, beat softened cream cheese and butter. Slowly add powdered sugar until smooth. Spread cake evenly with icing.

※ ※ ※ ※ ※ ※

Leave a space in your tummy for this one.

※ ※ ※ ※ ※ ※

Chapter 10
Cook-Keys

3 Meg Meringue Kisses

* * * * * * * * * *

Makes 5 dozen

3	egg whites	1	cup sugar
	Pinch salt	3/4	cup chopped nuts or mini chocolate chips
1	teaspoon vanilla		

Boot oven to 250 degrees F. In small mixing bowl or food processor, place egg whites and salt. Beat or process on high 10 minutes. Add vanilla and mix again. Add sugar in small quantities, mixing thoroughly.

Fold in nuts or chocolate chips. Drop batter from a teaspoon onto foil-covered cookie sheet. Bake for 45 minutes in center of oven. Let cool in dry place. Store in airtight container.

* * * * * *

A great snack while you're downloading — but watch those crumbs!

* * * * *

Bundle-Lemon Bars

* * * * * * * * * *

Serves 16-24 users

1	stick butter or margarine, softened	3	tablespoons lemon juice
1/4	cup powdered sugar		Rind of 1 lemon, grated
1	cup all-purpose flour	2	tablespoons all-purpose flour
1	cup granulated sugar		Powdered sugar for dusting top
2	eggs, well beaten		

Boot oven to 350 degrees F. In large mixing bowl, cream margarine and powdered sugar. Add flour and beat into a dough. Press mixture into the bottom of a greased 8x8-inch baking dish. Bake for 15 minutes.

In same bowl, beat granulated sugar, eggs, lemon juice, lemon rind and remaining flour until well blended. Pour mixture over baked crust and bake for 20 more minutes. Cool completely. Dust top lightly with powdered sugar. Cut into small squares and refrigerate.

Bundle

Choco-LAN Pecan Bars

Serves 24-36 users

1	box yellow cake mix	1	8-ounce package cream cheese, softened
2	eggs		
1	stick butter or margarine, melted	1	16-ounce package powdered sugar
1	cup chopped pecans	2	eggs
1	6-ounce package chocolate chips	1	teaspoon vanilla

Boot oven to 350 degrees F. Combine first 3 ingredients in large mixing bowl. Beat well. Spread mixture in well-greased 9x13-inch baking pan.

Sprinkle with chocolate chips and chopped pecans. Beat remaining ingredients until smooth and creamy. Pour over cake batter. Bake for 35-40 minutes. It will appear slightly sticky. Cool and cut into bars.

Chocolate Microchip Cookies

Makes about 60

2	sticks butter or margarine, softened	2-1/4	cups all-purpose flour
1/2	cup granulated sugar	1	teaspoon baking soda
1	cup brown sugar	1	12-ounce package mini chocolate chips
2	teaspoons vanilla	1	cup coarsely chopped walnuts
2	eggs		

Boot oven to 375 degrees F. In large mixing bowl, beat margarine, granulated sugar, brown sugar, vanilla and eggs until creamy. Beat in flour and baking soda. Stir in mini chocolate chips and nuts.

Drop by heaping tablespoons on ungreased cookie sheets. Bake for 8-10 minutes. Remove and cool on racks.

Clones? I thought you said cones!

This good without cooking? Go con-figure.

ConFig.Squares

Makes 16 squares

8	ounces dried figs	1	cup raisins
2	cups shelled pecans or walnuts	1	cup pitted dates

In food processor, combine all ingredients. Process until finely chopped. Press into a 8x8-inch buttered pan and cut into squares.

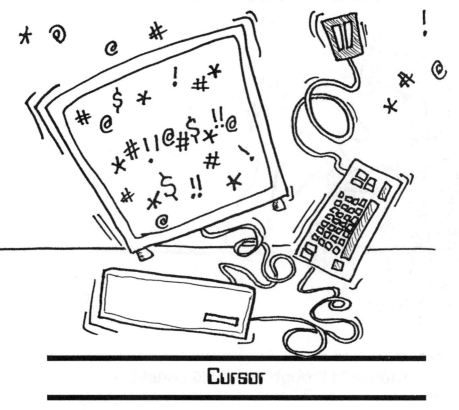

Cursor

Docu-Mint Microwave Brownies

Serves 16-24 users

2	squares unsweetened chocolate	1/2	cup flour
1/2	cup butter	2	teaspoons baking powder
3/4	cup sugar	1	teaspoon vanilla
2	eggs	3/4	cup mint chocolate chips
		1/2	cup chopped nuts, optional

In 2-cup glass measure, melt unsweetened chocolate and butter on high in microwave. Pour into large mixing bowl or food processor. Add sugar, eggs, flour, baking powder and vanilla. Mix well. Place in ungreased 8x8-inch microwave-safe dish.

Microwave on high for 3 minutes. Turn pan halfway and stir in chips and nuts. Continue cooking on high for 3 more minutes. Remove and let cool.

**Not a mint lover?
Use semi-sweet chocolate or
butterscotch chips instead.**

I/Oat Raisin Spacebars

* * * * * * * * * *

Serves 24-36 users

Filling:

2   cups raisins

1   14-ounce can sweetened condensed milk

1   tablespoon lemon juice

Crust and topping:

2   sticks butter or margarine, softened

1-1/3   cup brown sugar, firmly packed

1-1/2   teaspoons vanilla

2-1/2   cups rolled oats

1   cup all-purpose flour

1-1/2   cups walnuts, chopped

1/2   teaspoon baking soda

1/4   teaspoon salt

Boot oven to 375 degrees F. In medium saucepan, combine filling ingredients. Cook over medium heat until bubbles form. Remove from heat and set aside to cool slightly.

In large bowl, beat butter, sugar and vanilla until fluffy. Add remaining ingredients and blend with hands until evenly mixed and crumbly. Reserve 2 cups. Press remaining crumb mixture onto bottom of 9x13-inch greased pan. Spread raisin mixture to within 1/2 inch of edges. Top with remaining crumbs. Pat lightly.

Bake 25-35 minutes or until golden brown. Cool thoroughly. Cut into bars.

Mac-A-Roons

Serves 36-48 users

2	sticks butter or margarine, softened	1-1/4	cups all-purpose flour
1	cup brown sugar, packed	1	teaspoon baking soda
2	eggs	3	cups dry rolled oats
1/2	teaspoon almond extract	1-1/4	cups shredded coconut

Boot oven to 350 degrees F. Beat margarine and sugar until creamy. Add eggs and almond extract. Beat until fluffy.

In separate bowl, mix flour and baking soda. Add to creamed mixture and mix well. Stir in oats and coconut. Drop by rounded teaspoonfuls onto lightly-greased baking sheet. Bake for 10 minutes. Remove from baking sheet and cool on wire rack.

Oat-O-Exec.Batch Cookies

Makes 5-6 dozen

1-1/2	sticks butter or margarine, softened	1	teaspoon vanilla
1	cup brown sugar, packed	3	cups uncooked oats
1/2	cup granulated sugar	1	cup all-purpose flour
1	egg	1/2	teaspoon baking soda
1/4	cup water	1	cup raisins and/or chopped nuts, optional

Boot oven to 350 degrees F. Beat first 6 ingredients until creamy. In separate bowl, combine oats, flour and baking soda. Merge wet and dry ingredients and mix well. Stir in any optional items.

Drop by rounded teaspoonfuls onto greased baking sheet. Bake for 12-15 minutes.

Everyone will cluster to the kitchen when they smell these baking.

---

* * * * *

Pecan Cluster Bars

* * * * * * * * * *

Serves 24-36 users

Crust:

1-1/2	cups all-purpose flour
1/2	cup uncooked oats
1/3	cup brown sugar
1-1/2	sticks butter or margarine, softened

Filling:

4	eggs
1	cup pecans, coarsely chopped
1/2	cup brown sugar
1/4	teaspoon salt
1	cup light corn syrup
1	teaspoon vanilla
2	tablespoons all-purpose flour

Boot oven to 350 degrees F. Mix flour, oats and brown sugar. Cut in butter until mixture resembles coarse crumbs. Press mixture into greased 9x13-inch pan. Bake for 15 minutes.

In medium bowl, beat eggs slightly. Add remaining ingredients and mix thoroughly. Pour mixture into crust. Bake 30-35 minutes. Cool in pan on wire rack.

System 7-Layer Cookies

Serves 24-36 users

1	stick butter or margarine	1	cup shredded coconut
1-1/2	cups graham cracker crumbs	1	cup butterscotch chips
		1	cup pecans, chopped
1	cup semi-sweet chocolate chips	1	14-ounce can sweetened condensed milk

Boot oven to 350 degrees F. Melt butter in 9x13-inch baking pan. Sprinkle crumbs evenly over melted margarine. Layer chocolate chips, coconut, butterscotch chips and pecans.

Pour condensed milk evenly over top of layers. Bake for 30-35 minutes. While still warm, cut into 1-1/2-inch squares. Cool in pan on wire rack.

Get these cookies in your system.

Optimize

Chapter II
DOS-Serts

Banana Wafer Pudding

* * * * * * * * * *

Serves 12-16 users

2   *3-ounce packages vanilla pudding mix, prepared and cooled*

1   *12-ounce box vanilla wafers*

6   *ripe bananas, thinly sliced*

Layer bottom of 9x13-inch pan with vanilla wafers. Cover wafers with layer of bananas, then layer of pudding. Alternate layers, ending with pudding on top. Refrigerate for 4 hours or overnight.

* * * * * *

You'll go "Ba-nanos" over these!

---

* * * * *

Bananas DOS-ter

* * * * * * * * * *

Serves 8 users

1   *stick butter or margarine*

1   *16-ounce box light brown sugar*

4   *ripe bananas, peeled and quartered*

1/2   *cup bourbon, 100 proof*
Vanilla ice cream, scooped in balls in freezer

In medium skillet, melt margarine over low heat. Add brown sugar and cook until bubbly, stirring constantly. Add bananas, cooking slightly on one side. Turn and cook on other side.

Remove bananas from skillet and place in silver dish. Pour butter mixture, then bourbon over bananas. Flame. Place ice cream in individual serving dishes. Spoon 2 banana quarters and some sauce over ice cream.

Binary Cherry Puff

Serves 6-8 users

1	cup milk	1	21-ounce can cherry
2	eggs		pie filling
1/2	cup biscuit baking mix		
1/4	cup sugar		
1/2	teaspoon vanilla extract		
2	tablespoons butter or margarine, softened		

Boot oven to 400 degrees F. In large bowl, beat first 6 ingredients for 1 minute. Pour mixture into greased 10-inch pie pan or 11x7-inch baking pan. Spoon pie filling over top. Bake 30-35 minutes until golden brown.

F.A.T. Reducer: Use lowfat milk, diet margarine and light pie filling.

ALT: Try other fruit pie fillings.

Caramel F-LAN

❈ ❈ ❈ ❈ ❈ ❈ ❈ ❈ ❈ ❈

Serves 8 users

1-1/2	cups sugar	2	cups water
6	eggs, well beaten	1	teaspoon vanilla
1	14-ounce can sweetened condensed milk		

Stir sugar in heavy skillet over low heat until caramelized, being careful not to burn. Pour over bottom of ungreased, round 2-quart Pyrex dish. Set aside to cool.

Mix eggs, sweetened condensed milk, water and vanilla. Pour into caramel-coated dish. Place filled dish into shallow baking pan filled with one inch of water.

Bake at 325 degrees F for 1 hour or until knife inserted in middle comes out clean. Cool 30 minutes then refrigerate. Turn out on plate, caramel side up, before serving.

❈ ❈ ❈ ❈ ❈ ❈

F-LANtastic!!

❈ ❈ ❈ ❈ ❈ ❈

Chocolate Mous-se

* * * * * * * * * *

Serves 6-8 users

1   cup semi-sweet chocolate chips

1-1/4   cups light cream, scalded

2   egg yolks

Whipped cream

Semi-sweet chocolate shavings

Blend first 3 ingredients thoroughly in blender. Refrigerate mixture in one large bowl or individual dishes for 5 hours or overnight. To serve, top with whipped cream and semi-sweet chocolate shavings.

Cream Puff Shells

* * * * * * * * * *

Makes 5-6 dozen small or 24 large shells

1   cup water

1   stick butter or margarine

1   cup all-purpose flour

4   eggs, unbeaten

Boil water and butter in medium saucepan. Reduce heat and add flour all at once, stirring rapidly. Cook and stir until mixture thickens and leaves sides of pan. Place mixture in large mixing bowl. Add eggs one at a time, beating thoroughly after each. Beat until mixture looks satiny. Boot oven to 425 degrees F.

For small puffs, drop by teaspoonfuls onto ungreased baking sheet. Bake for 10-15 minutes or until done. For large puffs, drop by tablespoonfuls and bake for 15-20 minutes or until done.

Let cool. To fill, use a pastry bag or cut slit in side of each shell and spoon in. Chill filled puffs until ready to serve.

Suggested fillings: "Customize Custard", "Lemon CurdPerfect" or "Del-viled Eggheads" (filling only).

Crispy Apple PostScripty

Serves 8 users

4	cups apples, peeled and sliced	1	teaspoon ground cinnamon
1/4	cup water	1/2	cup uncooked oats
2	teaspoons lemon juice	2	tablespoons brown sugar
2	tablespoons brown sugar	2	tablespoons oil

Boot oven to 375 degrees F. Combine first 5 ingredients and mix well. Arrange mixture in well-greased 8x8-inch baking dish. Combine remaining ingredients and sprinkle over apples. Bake for 30 minutes or until topping is lightly browned.

A great postscript to any dinner.

Easy Pas-Tree Crust

* * * * * * * * * *

Makes 2 9-inch pie crusts

2   *cups all-purpose flour*   1/4   *cup cold water*

1   *teaspoon salt*   2   *9-inch pie plates*

1/2 *cup oil*

Mix flour and salt in bowl. Combine oil and water and mix into flour with fork. Form into 2 balls with hands. Cover with a cloth and let sit for 5 minutes. Roll out between sheets of waxed paper. Place rolled dough into pie plates.

For prebaked pie crusts, prick with fork and bake at 375 degrees F for 10-12 minutes.

Log on

Fragment Fruit Freeze

* * * * * * * * * *

Serves 4-6 users

4   bananas, peeled and
      sectioned

2   cups strawberries
      Sugar to taste

    In blender or food processor, blend bananas and berries. Add sugar to taste. Pour into ice cube trays and freeze. Remove fruit cubes from tray and blend again to make a lowfat, creamy dessert. Serve immediately.

    ALT: Substitute 2 cups of any peeled, seasonal fruit for the berries.

Freeze

136

Key-board Lime Pie

Makes 1 pie

3/4   cup fresh lime juice (key lime when in season)

1   14-ounce can sweetened condensed milk

4   eggs, separated

1   9-inch graham cracker pie crust

6   tablespoons sugar

Boot oven to 350 degrees F. In food processor or mixer, mix lime juice and condensed milk until smooth. Add 4 egg yolks and blend again. Beat one egg white until stiff and fold into mixture. Pour into unbaked pie crust.

To make meringue, beat remaining egg whites until stiff, gradually adding sugar. Spread over pie filling, sealing edges. Bake for 20-25 minutes until top is golden. Cool on wire rack and chill before serving, if desired.

Lemon CurdPerfect

Makes about 1-1/2 cups

1   cup sugar

4   tablespoons butter or margarine

1/3   cup fresh lemon juice

1   tablespoon grated lemon rind

3   eggs, beaten

In non-aluminum saucepan, combine first four ingredients. Stir over low heat until sugar dissolves. Strain eggs into hot mixture, stirring constantly. Cook, stirring constantly about 5 minutes until mixture thickens.

Pour into air-tight jar. Refrigerate up to 3 weeks. Use in layer cakes, tarts or as filling in "Cream Puffs Shells".

Microwave Customize Custard

* * * * * * * * * *

Serves 4-6 users

2	cups milk		2	tablespoons butter, melted
4	egg yolks		1	teaspoon vanilla
1/2	cup sugar		2	squares unsweetened chocolate, melted, optional
1/4	teaspoon salt			
3	tablespoons cornstarch			

Beat milk, egg yolks, sugar, salt and cornstarch. Pour into 2-quart microwave casserole dish. Microwave on high for 6-7 minutes, stirring with wire whisk after 3 minutes. When cooked, whisk in butter, vanilla and optional chocolate. Cover. Refrigerate until softly set.

* * * * * *

Everyone will want a PC of this!

* * * * * *

PC Peachy Cobbler

* * * * * * * * * *

Serves 6 users

1	stick butter or margarine, melted		1	cup sugar
1	cup all-purpose flour		1/2	teaspoon salt
1	teaspoon baking powder		1	cup milk
1	teaspoon baking soda		1	21-ounce can peach pie filling

Boot oven to 350 degrees F. Pour butter in 9x13-inch baking pan, tilting to cover bottom. In mixing bowl, thoroughly combine flour, baking powder, baking soda, sugar and salt. Stir in milk.

Pour batter evenly over melted butter. Add pie filling evenly on top of batter. Do not stir. Bake for 35-45 minutes until browned. Cool slightly before serving.

Pecan Pie A La Modem

* * * * * * * * * *

Makes 2 pies

1	stick butter or margarine	1/4	teaspoon salt
1/2	cup granulated sugar	1	cup chopped pecans
1/2	cup dark brown sugar	2	9-inch no-lard pie crusts, unbaked
1	cup light corn syrup		
4	eggs, beaten	2	cups pecan halves
2	teaspoons vanilla		Vanilla ice cream or frozen yogurt

Boot oven to 325 degrees F. Melt butter in saucepan over low heat. Stir in granulated sugar, brown sugar and corn syrup. Cook, stirring constantly until sugar is dissolved. Remove from heat. Stir in eggs, vanilla, salt and chopped pecans.

Pour equal amounts into pastry crusts. Arrange 1 cup pecans on top of each pie. Bake for 55-60 minutes. Let cool and top with vanilla ice cream.

Strawberry Fields Pie

* * * * * * * * * *

Serves 6 users

1	21-ounce can strawberry pie filling	1	cup self-rising flour
		1	cup sugar
1	stick butter or margarine, softened		

Boot oven to 325 degrees F. Place pie filling in well-greased 10x10-inch baking dish. In large bowl, mix butter, flour and sugar. Place over pie filling. Bake for 25-30 minutes or until top is nicely browned.

ALT: Substitute any fruit pie filling.

Toggle Noodle Kugel

Serves 6-8 users

3	eggs	2	cups creamed cottage cheese
1/2	cup sugar		
1	teaspoon vanilla	1	8-ounce package wide egg noodles, cooked and drained
1	teaspoon cinnamon		
1/4	cup melted butter	1	8-ounce can crushed pineapple
1/4	teaspoon salt		
1	cup sour cream	1/2	cup raisins
1/2	cup milk		

In large mixing bowl, beat all ingredients except noodles, pineapple and raisins. Stir noodles, pineapple and raisins into mixture. Pour into a buttered 2-quart baking dish. Bake at 350 degrees F for an hour or until top is golden.

F.A.T. Reducer: Use lowfat sour cream, lowfat cottage cheese and diet margarine.

Chapter 12
Holi-Data Treats

New Year's Eve Meg-Nog

●　　●　　●　　●　　●　　●　　●　　●　　●　　●

Serves 10-12 users

6　　eggs, separated

3/4　cup sugar

2-1/2 pints heavy cream

1-1/2 cups bourbon, dark rum or
　　　brandy, or to taste

Pinch salt

Pinch cream of tartar

Ground nutmeg

Beat egg yolks until thick and pale. Add sugar and beat until very thick. In separate bowl, beat 1 pint cream until medium thick and add to egg mixture. Add 1 more pint of cream, liquor and salt.

Beat egg whites and cream of tartar until they hold soft peaks. Fold into mixture. Beat remaining cream and fold in. Sprinkle with nutmeg and serve.

Hotkey Shortcut: Buy store-bought eggnog and get back on line!

F.A.T. Reducer: Substitute milk for second pint of cream.

User Friendly

Valentine Clip Hearts

● ● ● ● ● ● ● ● ● ●

Makes 1 large or 2 small tarts

3/4	cup uncooked oats	2	teaspoons oil
1	tablespoon walnuts	2	teaspoons apple juice
1/2	cup all-purpose flour	2	tablespoons honey
	Pinch salt	1	21-ounce can strawberry or
1/4	teaspoon ground cinnamon		cherry pie filling, chilled

Boot oven to 350 degrees F. In food processor or blender, grind oats and walnuts to a coarse meal. Combine oats mixture with flour, salt and cinnamon in a medium bowl. Stir in oil, juice and honey to form a soft dough.

Press dough evenly into bottom and sides of greased heart-shaped tart pan(s). Prick dough with fork several times and bake until golden, about 15-20 minutes. Let cool. Fill with pie filling and serve.

George Washington Cherry Tree-t

● ● ● ● ● ● ● ● ● ●

Serves 6 users

3/4	cup sifted flour	1	21-ounce can cherry pie
3/4	cup brown sugar		filling
6	tablespoons butter or		
	margarine, softened		

Boot oven to 375 degrees F. Mix together flour, brown sugar and butter until mixture resembles coarse meal. Set aside.

Place pie filling in 2-quart casserole. Spread crumb mixture on top. Bake 30-40 minutes, uncovered. Serve warm or let cool.

St. Paddy's Irish So-dBASE Bread

* * * * * * * * * *

Makes one round loaf

3/4	cup raisins	1/4	teaspoon baking soda
1	cup boiling water	1	cup buttermilk
2-3	cups unbleached white flour	3	tablespoons honey
1-1/2	teaspoons baking powder	1	tablespoon caraway seeds
1/2	teaspoon salt		

Boot oven to 350 degrees F. Cover raisins with boiling water for 10 minutes, then drain. In large bowl, mix together 2 cups flour, baking powder, salt and baking soda.

In separate bowl, blend buttermilk and honey. Stir in drained raisins and caraway seeds. Merge wet mixture into flour mixture a little at a time, to make a soft and just slightly sticky dough. If too sticky, add small amount of flour.

Knead dough for 1 minute. Form into round ball and place on greased baking sheet. Backslash top with knife. Bake for 40-50 minutes.

* * * * * *

Erin "GOTO" Bragh!

* * * * * *

Halloween Pump-Icon Pie

⚫ ⚫ ⚫ ⚫ ⚫ ⚫ ⚫ ⚫ ⚫ ⚫

Makes 2 pies

2	cups milk, scalded	1	teaspoon cinnamon
2	16-ounce cans pumpkin	3	eggs
1-1/4	cups sugar	2	9-inch no-lard pie crusts, unbaked
1/4	teaspoon salt		
1	teaspoon ground ginger		

Scald milk in medium saucepan. Set aside. Boot oven to 350 degrees F. Place pumpkin in mixing bowl. Add milk and remaining ingredients. Mix thoroughly.

Pour equal amounts of mixture into 2 pie crusts. Bake 45-60 minutes until toothpick or fork inserted in center comes out clean.

Thanksgiving Cranberry Corel-ish

⚫ ⚫ ⚫ ⚫ ⚫ ⚫ ⚫ ⚫ ⚫ ⚫

Makes about 5 cups

2	cups fresh cranberries	1	8-ounce can crushed pineapple, undrained
1	apple, unpeeled	1	cup sugar
2	oranges, peeled and seeded	1	cup chopped pecans

In food processor, chop cranberries, then place in large bowl. Next chop apple and oranges, adding to same bowl. Add remaining ingredients. Mix and chill.

F.A.T. Reducer: Reduce the nuts to 1/2 cup or omit altogether.

Christmas Disk-mas Dip

Makes about 3 cups

2 8-ounce packages cream cheese, softened

1 8 1/2-ounce can crushed pineapple, drained well

1-1/2 teaspoons salt or seasoning salt

1/4 cup each red and green bell pepper, chopped

2 tablespoons green onion tops, finely chopped

Whip cream cheese until fluffy. Add remaining ingredients and mix together.

Directory

Index

A

Appetizers
1 Meg-Plant Dip, 14
5.0 Layer Taco Dip, 13
Block Bean Dip, 12
Ched-Dir Corn Br-Ed, 98
Clip Art-ichoke Dip, 14
Cream Cheese Scroll-Ups, 15
Data Cream Dream Spread, 16
Del-viled Egg-heads, 17
Guaca-Modem Dip, 17
Hotkey Totsy Chutney, 18
Hum-Mouse Dip, 20
Mexi-Clone Taco Popcorn, 21
Microchip Salsa, 25
Nano-Nachos, 22
Nut Cheese Log-On, 23
Spicy Cheese Wafers, 26
Spinach CO-BOLs, 27
Stuffed Mush-ROM Caps, 28

Apple
Apple II Cake, 105
Crispy Apple PostScripty, 122
Excel-ery Waldorf Salad, 36
Mac Apple Torte, 111

Applesauce
Apple-DOS Cake, 104

Artichoke
Clip Art-ichoke Dip, 14

ASCII
ASCII Asparagus, 72
ASCII Broccoli Soup, 42

Asparagus
ASCII Asparagus, 72

Autoexec.bat
Oat-O-Exec.Batch Cookies, 125

Avocado
Creamy Avo-CAD-O Dressing, 34
Guaca-Modem Dip, 17

B

Backup
Pineapple Backup-Side Down Cake,
114

Banana
Ba-Nano Nut Bread, 97
Banana Wafer Pudding, 130
Bananas DOS-ter, 130
Fragment Fruit Freeze, 136

Basil
Compress-to Pesto, 62
dBASIL Tomato Salad, 35

Batch
Gaz-Batch-O, 49

Beans
Adobean Soup, 44
Bean-ary Salad, 32
Binary Beanery Chili, 86
Block Bean Dip, 12
Excel-Lentil Soup, 48
Turbo-ritos, 85
VGA Veggie Chili, 94

Beverages
New Year's Eve Meg Nog, 142

Binary
Bean-ary Salad, 32
Binary Beanery Chili, 86
Binary Cherry Puff, 131

Biscuits
Low Density Biskettes, 99

Block
Block Bean Dip, 12
Stir-Fried Block-oli, 80

Breads
B-RAM Muffins, 96
Ba-Nano Nut Bread, 97
Ched-Dir Corn Br-Ed, 98
Low Density Biskettes, 99
Pineapple Zoom-chini Bread, 100
Pumpkin Rais-Input Nut Bread, 102

Quick Cheese Scrolls, 102
St. Paddy's Irish So-dBASE Bread,
144

Broccoli
ASCII Broccoli Soup, 42
Stir-Fried Block-oli, 80

Brownies
Docu-Mint Microwave Brownies,
123

Bulghur Wheat
Binary Beanery Chili, 86
Enchi-Load-DOS, 83
Hacker Helper, 82
Ta-CO-BOL Tacos, 84
Tab-ouli Salad, 39
Turbo-ritos, 85

Bundle
Bundle-Lemon Bars, 118

Burritos
Turbo-ritos, 85

C
CAD
Creamy Avo-CAD-O Dressing, 34

Cakes
Apple II Cake, 105
Apple-DOS Cake, 104
Binary Cherry Puff, 131
Cinna-Mono Crumb Coffee Cake,
108
Cinnamon 'Floppy', 106
Cut and Taste Coffee Cake, 109
G-RAM Cracker Crust, 112
Gooey Butter Spreadsheet Cake,
110
Mac Apple Torte, 111
PC Peachy Cobbler, 138
Peach-Tree Cheesecake, 113
Pineapple Backup-Side Down
Cake, 114
Spicebar Cake, 116

Caps
Stuffed Mush-ROM Caps, 28

Caramel
Caramel F-LAN, 132

Cauliflower
Curry Cauli-Floppy Soup, 43

CD
Spicy Sesame CD Noodles, 70

Celery
8.0 Layer Potluck Salad, 30
Excel-ery Waldorf Salad, 36

Cheese
Baked Macro-ni Casserole, 52
Ched-Dir Corn Br-Ed, 98
Command-icotti, 61
Fett-Icon-E Alfredo, 63
Hack Jack Cheese Grits, 55
Lowfat Laser-gna, 87
Nano-Nachos, 22
Noodles ROM-ano, 67
PC Shells, 68
Quick 'N' Quiche, 57
Quick Cheese Scrolls, 102
Spicy Cheese Wafers, 26
Zu-Key-ni Pie, 58

Cherry
Binary Cherry Puff, 131
George Washington Cherry Tree-t,
143
Valentine Clip Hearts, 143

Chickpeas
Hum-Mouse Dip, 20
Middle Eastern Fela-File, 92

Chili
Binary Beanery Chili, 86
VGA Veggie Chili, 94

Chocolate
Choco-LAN Pecan Bars, 120
Chocolate Microchip Cookies, 121
Chocolate Mous-se, 133
System 7-Layer Cookies, 127

Nerd Notes

Nerd Notes

Other books available from Strawberry Patch:

"For Popcorn Lovers Only"
by Diane Pfeifer ($9.95)
Over 100 fun popcorn recipes, cartoons and trivia as seen on "Regis & Kathie Lee" and "The Home Show". Give one to the popcorn lover in your life.

"Gone With The Grits Gourmet Cookbook"
by Diane Pfeifer ($9.95)
Not just for Southerners or breakfast anymore! Grits go gourmet in 135 unique recipes, with grits quiz and funny cartoons. As seen on "CBS This Morning" and "Cookin' USA".

"The Pregnant Husband's Handbook"
by Jeff Justice ($5.95)
All those uncomfortable questions women pose during pregnancy with hilarious multiple-choice answers and cartoons. Finally a gift for that forgotten male!

"You Know You're A New Parent When. . ."
by Jeff Justice & Diane Pfeifer ($5.95)
Perfect for all new parents. A funny look at those unforgettable moments when baby arrives ... and STAYS! Laugh along with these cartooned truisms of early parenthood.

"Jeff Justice's Comedy Workshoppe Jokebook"
by Jeff Justice ($5.00)
The author, also a professional comedian and standup comedy teacher has compiled the "best of" rib-ticklers from his past students. Great when you (or someone else) needs a laugh!

To order, call toll-free: 1-800-875-7242